Paul Hymans

Makers
of the
Modern
World

Paul Hymans
Belgium
Sally Marks

HAUS HISTORIES

First published in Great Britain in 2010 by
Haus Publishing Ltd
70 Cadogan Place
London SW1X 9AH
www.hauspublishing.com

A CIP catalogue record for this book
is available from the British Library

ISBN 978-1-905791-81-1

Series design by Susan Buchanan
Typeset in Sabon by MacGuru Ltd
Printed in Dubai by Oriental Press
Map by Martin Lubikowski, ML Design, London

Contents

Prologue: Hymans at Paris

At the Paris Peace Conference on the evening of 5 February 1919, the League of Nations Commission was debating the composition of the future League of Nations Council, where originally only the Great Powers – Britain, France, Italy, Japan and the United States – were to sit. Vociferous protests from Paul Hymans of Belgium gained two seats for all the lesser states together. As his further protests met with general opposition from Great Power representatives, Hymans shouted: *What you propose is a revival of the Holy Alliance of unhallowed memory!* Ultimately he gained four seats for the lesser states, a signal victory achieved at considerable cost in hostility.

In this, Paul Hymans was a typical representative of a small state seeking a voice, albeit in his inexperience an unusually outspoken and tactless one who often outraged those he needed to charm. Yet Belgium was unusual in its past and, as the Great Powers soon reluctantly had to admit, distinctive in other ways in its present circumstances and in its future. Belgium and Hymans were unrealistic in their expectations of the Paris Peace Conference and disappointed at Belgium's limited gains from the Versailles Treaty. But as Paul Hymans gained experience and wisdom, he and Belgium learned together in the years that followed what life and diplomacy amid the Great Powers meant for a small state.

Note: The most common English-language usage is employed for Belgian place names. Where that is the French version, the Flemish counterpart is given in parentheses at first use. Example: Ypres (Ieper).

Paul Hymans was the Belgian Minister for Foreign Affairs three times. He was representative to the Paris Peace Conference in 1919

I
The Life and the Land

1

The Crossroads of Europe

Belgium is an ancient land, populated as early as 150,000 BC and later one of the three parts of Julius Caesar's Gaul, but it is a comparatively recent state, dating from the 1830s. Whether it is also a nation remains unclear, for it is chiefly comprised of two peoples: the Teutonic Flemings to the north who speak Dutch and dialects thereof, and the Celtic Walloons to the south who speak French and its dialects. Brussels, located within Flanders, is a bilingual zone. From the outset, there was also a small German-speaking element in the borderlands.

For centuries of modern history, foreign powers ruled the Belgians. The last of these was the United Kingdom of the Netherlands created after the Napoleonic Wars to provide a barrier against France. The Grand Duchy of Luxembourg became a personal possession of King William I, though within the German Confederation and its customs union. The Belgian-Dutch marriage was not happy. Overwhelmingly Catholic and localistic Belgians resented Dutch Protestantism and centralisation. William I's attempt to 'Dutchify' the schools alarmed Walloons and Flemish elites who feared their children educated in Dutch would be cut off from the learned professions. An economic downturn hurt urban workers and businessmen. Dissatisfaction was such that the two main political factions, Catholic and Liberal, called a truce to unite against the Dutch. Yet no revolution was planned.

A spontaneous uprising leading to independence was sparked on 25 August 1830, barely a month after the July Revolution in France, by a performance at the Théâtre de la Monnaie in the heart of Brussels of an opera celebrating a Neapolitan rebellion against oppression. Excited crowds burst forth into the summer night singing the key aria, set to the tune of the *Marseillaise*:

What danger can a slave incur?
Better to die than live in slavery.
Throw off the yoke of the oppressor
And let the stranger fall under our blows.
Sacred love of country gives us fortitude and audacity.
My country gave me life,
I shall give it liberty! [1]

This incitement spread to passers-by and then to the city's workers. Suddenly there was an uprising, which succeeded because the timid Dutch military commander withdrew his troops. As protest against misrule became a national revolution, the upper middle class took charge. Independence was declared in an orderly fashion on 4 October and a National Congress elected a month later.

At this juncture, the Great Powers intervened, meeting in London. Almost immediately the Whig Viscount Palmerston became British Foreign Secretary. He chiefly wanted to prevent war or French control of Belgium. Russia and to a degree Austria were preoccupied with revolution in Poland, Prussia overburdened with debt, and Louis Philippe of France too precarious on his new throne to do other than follow Britain's lead. Thus when the Belgian National Congress deposed the House of Nassau and opted for a constitutional monarchy, the London Conference obligingly declared the union dissolved and recognised Belgian independence in January 1831.

The Belgians wrote the Continent's most liberal, but not most democratic, constitution on the British model. It provided a two-chamber Parliament elected by the propertied classes, separation of church and state, freedom of religion, assembly and the press, and local autonomy. The monarch, who was and is inaugurated, would be King of the Belgians, reigning over the people, but not feudal lord of the land.* Though his influence was great, his power was limited to commanding the army in wartime. As King, the National Congress wisely elected Leopold, the German uncle of young Princess Victoria of Great Britain. He married a daughter of the new French King, Louis Philippe. Heirs to the throne followed. Leopold I (1831–65) was handsome, dignified, shrewd and well-versed in European power politics, of which his people knew little. As his looks faded with age, he became pompous and egotistical, but on the whole he served Belgium well.

After his installation, Holland sent an army, which France expelled with British consent. British pressure then induced French withdrawal. The London Conference achieved an

---

*When a King of Belgium dies, the throne becomes vacant. Within ten days, the heir appears before the two legislative Houses united in joint session, swears an oath to the Constitution and the laws of the Belgian people, and thus becomes King (Articles 90, 91, Belgian Constitution, http://www.servat.unibe.ch/law/icl/be00000_.html).

armistice and a document outlining bases of separation, which Belgium reluctantly accepted but Holland did not. Thus Luxembourg and the southernmost Dutch province of Limburg along the Meuse (Maas) River were governed as part of Belgium until the final settlement in 1839, when half of Catholic Limburg and slightly less than half of Luxembourg (the remnant of which reverted to its former status) were lost. The Kingdom was now slightly larger than present-day Albania. Belgium had aspired vainly as well to Flemish Zeeland, which controlled the south bank of the Scheldt River from Antwerp to the sea but, unlike Luxembourg and Limburg, had not participated in the Belgian revolt. In later years, Belgians complained that their country had been truncated at all three corners of its territory.

The three treaties of 19 April 1839 formed an interrelated whole. The Belgian-Dutch Treaty, consisting of the final revised 24 Articles of Separation, specified Belgian borders, declared the Kingdom perpetually neutral and contained economic clauses, the most important of which guaranteed access to the sea through Dutch waters for Antwerp and access to the Scheldt through Flemish Zeeland for the Ghent-Terneuzen Canal. Antwerp was to be a purely commercial port. Identical treaties of the five Great Powers with Belgium and the Netherlands annexed those 24 Articles and placed them under guarantee of the five major signatories: Britain, France, Austria, Prussia and Russia.

QUINTUPLE TREATY WITH BELGIUM
'[The Five Powers] declare that the Annexed Articles ... are considered as having the same force and value as if they were textually inserted in the present treaty, and that they are thus placed under the guarantee of their said Majesties.

ANNEX
Article VII. Belgium ... shall form an independent and perpetually neutral state. It shall be bound to observe such neutrality toward all other states.'[2]

In imposing compulsory neutrality, the Powers were trying to insulate the 'Crossroads of Europe', a broad plain between the marshy basins of the Rhine and Meuse Rivers and the heavily forested Ardennes uplands, where so many merchants and especially so many armies had marched through the centuries. Though Belgians disliked a number of treaty clauses, neutrality was not much of an issue, partly because events between 1831 and 1839 had established Belgium's right to defend itself. Indeed, the European consensus was that it had an obligation to do so. A greater problem for Belgians and others was the nature of the guarantee. If one of the Guarantors violated it, invading Belgium, were the others obligated to come to its defence militarily or merely not to participate in the violation? Belgian leaders preferred the more protective view, as usually did Palmerston.

No clarification occurred during the reign of Leopold I, but the issue arose soon after his son's accession. Leopold II (1865–1909) was a figure of large virtues and larger faults. Among the latter were his scandalous private life, his perhaps excessive ambitions for his little Kingdom and his exploitative policies in the Congo Free State, which was his personal possession. As to the former, he modernised Brussels, creating its sweeping boulevards, gave wholehearted support to the enterprises of Belgian financiers and engineers in distant corners of the globe, and concerned himself with the Kingdom's defences, which were in good repair until after 1870.

From 1866 until late 1870, Belgium's future was in jeopardy. The crisis arose because in 1866 Napoleon III of France sought compensation for the Prussian acquisition of Schleswig-Holstein after the 1864 Danish War and for his neutrality in the approaching Austro-Prussian War. The Prussian Prime Minister, Prince Otto von Bismarck, dangled a draft treaty for French acquisition of Belgium and Luxembourg which he enticed the French envoy to put into writing on embassy stationery, and then he stalled. Accordingly, Napoleon sought to buy Luxembourg, which had a Prussian garrison in its capital. Dutch consent was withdrawn after Bismarck announced Prussian alliances with South German states not part of his new North German Confederation (which acceded to the 1839 Treaties). Leopold II hoped to gain Luxembourg in this fluid situation, but his Liberal Cabinet deemed any move to that end too risky and Luxembourg too full of potential Catholic voters, so Belgium did nothing. As the crisis passed, the Great Powers neutralised Luxembourg and removed the Prussian garrison by the Treaty of London of 11 May 1867, which imposed perpetual neutrality on the Grand Duchy under a guarantee of the Powers which specifically did not oblige them to act upon its violation.

In July 1870, the Franco-Prussian War broke out. To gain diplomatic support Bismarck released the 1866 draft treaty to *The Times*. Britain signed pacts in August with France and Prussia citing the 1839 Treaties and pledging to protect Belgium against either. Belgium prepared to defend itself. But French defeat was so swift that the Belgian crisis passed; there was no other threat before 1914. The new Germany was universally deemed to have assumed the North German Confederation's obligation to the 1839 Treaties. Even so, as late as 1913 when German intentions were widely suspected, the British Foreign Secretary, Sir Edward Grey, mused: 'What we had to consider, and it was a somewhat embarrassing question, was what it would be desirable and necessary for us, as one of the Guarantors of Belgian neutrality, to do if Belgian neutrality was violated by any Power.' [3]

After 1870, Belgium considered neutrality and the guarantee sufficient to ensure its safety, neglected its army and turned its attention to internal concerns. It developed a competent diplomatic corps whose energies were largely devoted to commercial matters and industrial projects abroad to be constructed by Belgian firms. On the whole, Belgium remained outside the main currents of European diplomacy: insulated, isolated and preoccupied with domestic issues.

As early as 1834, Belgium decided to construct the Continent's first national rail network. This contributed to economic development, primarily in Wallonia, where the iron and steel industry surged. Flanders remained agricultural and impoverished. Walloon industrial maturity was reached by 1870, and Belgian firms expanded overseas, which benefited Antwerp. The economy continued to grow, often at the expense of the workers whose conditions were miserable. Little Belgium became Europe's fourth industrial power and the world's fifth-ranked trading nation.

Meanwhile, Belgium had created its institutions. Initially, all governmental ones, including law courts, were francophone, for French was declared the sole national language at independence though Flemings outnumbered Walloons. In an era when language was partly a matter of class, aristocrats, wealthy businessmen and the learned professions (all francophone) dominated the tiny electorate and the government nationally and in the provinces. Gradually Flemish gained acceptance in more government activities, but full language equality was not achieved before 1914.

The revolutionary year of 1848 did much to establish Belgium as a real state in European eyes. It experienced unrest but, to the envy of others, no revolution. A judicious combination of political reforms, including a widening of the franchise, and public works to create jobs and wages quieted the country. The latter were financed by a forced loan imposed upon the most prosperous firms, enabling Belgium to proceed smoothly on its chosen way.

Of the two original political factions, the Liberals became a political party in 1846. The more conservative Catholics became one in all but name soon thereafter. They were subject to intermittent Vatican influence, chiefly concerned with religious control of education and social programmes and were strongest in rural areas, especially Flanders. The Liberals, dedicated to secular education in state schools, were primarily urban and anchored in Wallonia. They attracted secular-minded or non-practising Catholics, those of other faiths or none, and Freemasons. During Belgium's first 50 years, the two parties alternated in power, debating the language question, the schools, the suffrage, and occasionally the army. Despite dissatisfaction over these issues, no separatist movement developed.

An 1878 Liberal electoral victory led to a law the next year excluding religion from primary schools. The reaction was so intense that the Catholics won the 1884 election and repealed the law. They governed uninterruptedly until the cataclysm of 1914. There was never another purely Liberal ministry and no Liberal participation in a Cabinet until the war. In addition, the Belgian Workers' (Socialist) Party was organised in 1877 and, after electoral reform in 1893, outstripped the Liberals in the next election. Thereafter Socialists and Liberals alternated as the second party.

The Socialists had been a movement before creating a political party. As labour unions were initially illegal, they formed associations to meet the needs of workers. Though some, such as bakeries to provide bread, were commercial, many, such as clinics, were social in nature. As a broad web of Socialist social services developed, the Catholics created their own counterparts. Thus was born the distinctive Belgian phenomenon of pillarization, wherein an individual could and did have his social needs met virtually from cradle to grave by his political party.

Suffrage was a constant political issue, particularly for Socialists, in the latter part of the 19th century. After a strike in 1893, constitutional reform brought universal suffrage for males at age 25, but with plural voting. This benefited the Socialists somewhat, and they cut into the Liberal base in Wallonia, but the law chiefly favoured the rich and the rural, primarily the dominant Catholics. To protect minorities, proportional representation was introduced in 1899 and saved the Liberal Party from insignificance. After a general strike in 1913, a revision of the electoral system to provide equal suffrage was promised, but did not occur before Belgium was engulfed in war.

Meanwhile, the Parliament had faced the question of the Congo Free State, which Leopold II had retained because the Great Powers did not wish to go to war over its possession. In 1890, in return for a state loan, the King had ceded to Belgium the right to acquire the Congo after ten years, and in 1895 financial embarrassment led him to try to cede it to the state at once. Belgians emphatically did not want a colony, and the outcry was so intense that the King withdrew the cession. In 1901, the parliament voted not to exercise its right to take the Congo Free State. Soon thereafter, however, international protest over Leopold's mistreatment of the African inhabitants became so acute that in 1908 Belgium reluctantly took over the Congo to end the abuses. This it did, substituting a regime which was intensely paternalistic and not conducive to creation of an indigenous elite but which otherwise provided better conditions than those in other African colonies.

After 1900, Wallonia began to decline economically and Flanders to industrialise, starting a long trend. As the Flemings gained more language rights, a literary renaissance occurred. Belgium was densely populated and immensely prosperous, but increasingly uneasy, for Europe was lurching from crisis to crisis. Thus the deplorable state of the nation's army and its antiquated conscription system became an issue, as intermittently in the past. Most Belgians saw no need for a neutral state to spend money on fortifications and equipment, and attracting able young men to a career in an army which seemed never likely to fight was difficult. Conscription had long been by national lottery, but those chosen to serve could purchase substitutes if they could afford to do so. This was popular not only with the propertied classes but also with Flemish farmers willing to send a son to service in order to gain a financial stake. Thus the Catholic party clung to the system, which produced a substantial Flemish majority among the rank-and-file alongside a francophone officer corps.

The old King persisted. Finally, a December 1909 law ended the lottery and substitutions, decreed one son must serve from each family (with many exemptions) and shortened the term of service. Leopold signed it on his deathbed. This was necessary but not sufficient, in view of diplomatic hints that Germany expected war with France and the existence of nine major rail lines between France and Germany through Belgium, plus another running from the German military camp at Elsenborn to the Belgian border. The new King, Albert I (1909–34) continued his predecessor's efforts. As the international situation worsened, opposition declined.

The Liberal leader, Paul Hymans, was prophetic: *How*

would it be, if some morning the bugle of war sounded at the frontier? ... Let us imagine, in a terrible dream, invasion, occupation ... and after the horrors of the lost battle, the forced labour, the requisitioning, the humiliations, and the shame![4] The 1913 bill passed, providing universal conscription and a much enlarged force, but the reforms were incomplete and the army in awkward transition when the bugle of war sounded.

2
The First Career

The parentage of Paul Hymans, though distinctive in its Calvinism on both sides, blended the two main ethnicities of Belgium. His paternal grandfather was a Dutch-born physician who arrived in Belgium before the 1830 Revolution. His father Louis was a member of the upper bourgeoisie, a man of letters, a journalist, a history professor, a member of the Belgian Academy and a Liberal deputy representing Brussels in the Chamber. His mother came of an old aristocratic Walloon family. Their only son was born at Ixelles (Elsene), a well-to-do francophone commune (borough) within Greater Brussels, on 23 March 1865 shortly before the long reign of Leopold II began.

As a child, young Paul was tutored at home by his father, who instilled his love of politics in his son. Louis's interests were purely intellectual and he had no experience of business; he trained his son accordingly. Louis also had little interest in religion. Paul received his religious instruction from his mother and from the Protestant secondary schools he attended. As a university student, he lost his faith but not his Christian morality; ultimately he became a spiritually inclined deist. At the Free University of Brussels, a Liberal stronghold which proclaimed its independence of both church and state, he attended the Faculty of Law but also studied philosophy and showed an interest in politics.

When Paul was 19, his father died, leaving him the sole support of his mother and sister. Family connections obtained for him a position as assistant librarian to the Chamber of Representatives, which enabled him to continue his studies. He gained his degree with distinction, entered the Brussels bar, practiced law, and became a correspondent, as his father had been, for *La Meuse*, but remained a parliamentary librarian until he entered the Chamber himself in 1900. Thus he gained an unrivalled knowledge of the workings and history of the Belgian Parliament. Meanwhile, he completed his father's unfinished volumes, designed and taught a course in the new School of Politics and Social Science at the Free University of Brussels, as he continued to do until the First World War, as well as another course in parliamentary history, and wrote for other journals, including *L'Indépendance Belge*. This multiplicity of activities was not unusual among educated Belgians, though more extensive than most. Hymans wrote well and often, for he joined many cultural and educational organisations, becoming an officer of some and producing speeches or articles for appropriate occasions, as he did throughout his life. From the first, he had no interest in material wealth and avoided the world of business.

Hymans became a disciple of the Liberal leader Walther Frère-Orban. When a group of Liberals, including Frère-Orban, established a journal to combat the movement for universal male suffrage, it was unofficially edited by Hymans and his close lifelong friend Adolphe Max, later Burgomaster of Brussels. Hymans thought universal male suffrage was premature in a country with a high illiteracy rate. He soon changed his mind, though stressing the need for compulsory education to go with the vote.

In 1898 Hymans married Thérèse Goldschmidt in church. The marriage was happy (*the light of my life*[1]) but childless. The means she brought to the union enabled her husband to remain indifferent to material matters, to indulge his taste for elegant attire, and to build his sole luxury, a gracious but not grand house facing the Brussels Park. Mme Hymans strongly supported her husband's career, engaging in activities appropriate to the wife of a prominent man. For example, during the First World War, she facilitated correspondence between troops on the Yser (IJzer) front and families in occupied Belgium. When her husband became Envoy to Great Britain, she addressed the welfare of the Belgian Refugee community there.

The advent of universal male suffrage with plural voting favoured the extremes of opinion and proved disastrous for the Liberal Party. Thus Hymans and others became proponents of proportional representation. As an expert in comparative public law, he knew the dangers of such a system but thought the advantages outweighed them for the Liberal Party and to preserve existing laws. Thanks to this alteration in the electoral system, which took effect in 1899, Hymans was elected in 1900 at the age of 35 to the Chamber as a deputy from Brussels, serving as the voice of the capital's intellectual elite until his death in 1941. When first elected, he was already well known to his party, especially for his talent and oratory, which was always carefully prepared, and from the outset he was considered a 'rising star'. This particular star shot up with meteoric speed: in 1903 Paul Hymans, not yet 40 years old, became leader of the Liberal Party.

The new leader was a small and fragile-looking man who dominated by intellectual power and parliamentary skill. A long neck and narrow face with a moustache and a very full head of hair sat atop a nervous and delicate body. His education had been purely cerebral. He had no interest in sports and took no exercise aside from walking in the park, invariably with cigarette in hand. He never served in the army and lacked manual dexterity or skills. Hymans was considered the most aristocratic of the upper bourgeoisie and was noted for the elegance of his attire, manners, taste and language. He was charming, kind, and generous to most, though tending to lash out at fools and those he deemed wicked. A man of intense rectitude whose motto was *nothing dubious*, he savoured an artful witticism and occasionally produced one, but was uncomfortable with off-colour humour. Max, known for his amours and Rabelaisian tales, kept that side of his personality from his close friend. Hymans was an intensely private man whose memoirs are entirely diplomatic, not personal.

Paul Hymans was an idealist who understood the limits of the possible. A model of clarity and probity, he loathed intrigue and hypocrisy. He was religious in a nonsectarian spiritual sense and always optimistic, saying: *To live is to hope.*[2] He was exceptionally honest in public and in private, a characteristic not necessarily always advantageous in a politician and a diplomatist. Patience was not his strong suit. He could be testy and touchy, especially with Liberal members in Parliament or party meetings, and became nervous if faced with pointless oratory or discussion. If angry, he made no effort to conceal his wrath.

Hymans avoided all matters commercial and stayed so far from the business world that he knew little of economics, a subject not considered important during his schooldays. In later years, he ran the Foreign Trade Department of the Foreign Ministry capably but was disconcerted by the growing state involvement in the economy. He could not handle technical discussions of economic issues in the Cabinet and resisted their very terminology. Though not indifferent to lower-class welfare, he lived a life isolated from social problems and from the popular agitation which he much disliked. He was also isolated from Flemish speakers but, unlike most francophones of his era, was neither indifferent nor hostile to the language question. In 1913 he and Max began to study Flemish, an unusual step ended by the war.

> Liberalism is the expression of an eternal aspiration which cannot be compressed in the human soul: the aspiration for freedom.
>
> PAUL HYMANS[3]

For Paul Hymans, liberalism was a conviction and a philosophy, not just a political programme. At the core of his liberalism was the belief that ideas are dominant. He opposed all constraints and limitations, arguing that human beings wish to be free and resting on the power of the individual will and the importance of free will. For Hymans, the goals of liberalism were man's happiness and the greatest possible freedom to the individual in all spheres of human activity insofar as this was compatible with the rights of others and public order.

For the 19th-century liberal, reason – without prejudging – was the guide to the truth. Hymans rested heavily on the French Revolution's Declaration of the Rights of Man and the Citizen of 26 August 1789. The state was a political institution to maintain a social order of maximum tolerance based on personal liberty, including freedom of conscience, opinion, doctrine and discussion. As a humanist, Hymans believed in justice and moral progress, combining classical wisdom and Christian morality. He had faith in human values, in the dignity of man, in the creative powers of man's intelligence and in the moral faculties of man's soul. He wanted to protect these attributes from both religious intolerance and the potential despotism of the state.

Belgian liberals saw liberty as a superior state of social life which one must earn. They stressed freedom of doctrine, moderation and tolerance, fearing that in religion and philosophy narrower rules would lead to oppression and arbitrariness. They opposed extreme inequality, seeking balance. Hymans personally favoured an aristocracy of thought, morals and intelligence which he deemed necessary to society, especially in a democracy. He deplored the declining civic activity of Belgium's hereditary aristocracy and the lack of intellectual interest of most of the middle class.

He thought liberty required the active responsibility of every citizen. Individual rights were paramount but must be harmonised with those of the state, whose powers should be limited and whose purpose was to ensure order and freedom. Social reforms were needed, partly to prevent excess regulation, and state intervention was necessary for the sake of general interests, especially those of the masses. Hymans sought middle-class solidarity and awareness of the needs of the poor to curb excess bourgeois individualism and egotism. He respected the working class and wanted to improve its lot, favouring social legislation. But compulsory membership in trade unions would be a violation of individual liberty. Solidarity meant freedom for others in society. Where some might be indifferent or rely on charity, Belgian liberals stressed the idea of solidarity and an insurance system.

Hymans was dedicated to democracy, fearing only its misuse. He favoured capitalism with its abuses redressed. He opposed all ideological systems and rejected all doctrinal servitudes, declaring no monopolies on the truth existed. He condemned materialism, Marxism and even Belgium's mild socialism, wherein he saw a danger of absolutism, the domination of a single class and dictatorship by a committee. He opposed any form of authoritarianism, thinking the Roman Catholic Church preached submission and docility and autocracies sacrificed the individual to society and the state.

Like other late 19th-century intellectuals, Hymans believed in the idea of progress and had enormous admiration for science, which would bring continual progress. That depended on education, which Belgian liberals insisted should be free and compulsory. Since the state should be neutral in the clash of ideas, instruction in state schools should be secular. In fact, compulsory education was enacted by Parliament in 1914, but the Catholic votes necessary for passage ensured that state and church schools were both subsidised.

The Liberal Party heartily supported the old liberal formula: 'The teacher at the school, the priest at the church, the mayor at the town hall.' This harmless-sounding slogan was explosive in Belgian politics, where the question of religious instruction in state schools recurred frequently and where in 1880 Pope Leo XIII condemned Belgian liberalism. Hymans and the Liberal Party did not wish to destroy religion, but wanted it separated from politics, for the civil power should be independent, especially of religion. Hymans himself was anticlerical in the political sense, but not otherwise.

Liberals ardently supported the Belgian Constitution, an exceptionally liberal document providing equality before the law, civil liberties and freedom of religion. Hymans preferred a representative constitutional monarchy for Belgium, with no divisive elections for the head of state. Besides, having a prince was traditional. When plural voting generated a tendency to extremes, which Liberals abhorred, they opted for proportional representation to prevent oppression by the majority. Bowing to political necessity, Hymans accepted the prospect of equal (not plural) manhood suffrage in 1906, though he personally favoured preference to age, family responsibility and education.

When Hymans became the Liberal leader in 1903, his first task was to unify his party, which was sharply split between doctrinaires and progressives. As the acknowledged leader of the moderate Liberals, he succeeded in this. His party reached agreement on compulsory education, compulsory military service without lottery or substitution, and improving the lot of the workers. No combination on these questions with the Socialists emerged, though the Liberals sought one. The leader's next task was to enlarge the Liberal contingent in the Chamber. Here, too, Hymans succeeded, gaining more seats in each election. When a parliamentary election was suddenly called for June 1912, the Liberals anticipated victory and he expected to become Prime Minister. But the Catholics managed to retain office by exploiting the fear of socialism. Thereafter, the opportunity having passed, Hymans was less ambitious for himself, concentrating more on Belgium's safety and welfare. As strikes mounted over electoral reform, he sought social peace and improvement of the nation's defences.

In an imperialist era, Hymans favoured Belgium obtaining colonies. He wanted to take the Congo in 1901. In 1908 he cooperated with Leopold II over transfer of the Free State to Belgium and helped to write the law governing colonial administration. He also backed the old King's efforts toward military reform, serving on the parliamentary committee which ended the lottery and substitutions in favour of requiring military service by one son per family. All Liberals and Socialists and some Catholics voted for it. But Hymans knew it was not enough and objected to shortening the term of service, a stand which made him unpopular. Through continuing battles over religious instruction in the schools, he sensed the danger ahead and worked with Albert I to strengthen the nation's defences.

When the First World War broke over Belgium in August 1914, Hymans had been a member of a minority party for 30 years and its leader for more than a decade. He had never held ministerial office or attended Crown Councils. Suddenly everything changed. On 2 August 1914, he became a Minister of State, participating in Crown Councils. After a three-party mission to the United States, he soon became Belgium's envoy to Great Britain despite his lack of prior diplomatic experience. In 1916, he entered the Cabinet, and on 1 January 1918 became Minister of Foreign Affairs which thereafter was always his post of choice. Paul Hymans had found his métier.

3
In the Crucible

Belgium's traumatic experience in the First World War derived from its location, terrain and especially Germany's single plan for a general European war. The Franco-Russian defensive alliance of 1894 faced the Reich with the prospect of a two-front war. To avoid that, its General Staff devised a scheme to take advantage of Russia's slow mobilisation, owing to its vast size and inadequate railways, by hurling most of the German army into France via the speediest route – through Belgium, whose 'chocolate soldiers' would melt at once. Germany would defeat France within six weeks, and then turn, using its excellent railways, to face Russia. This plan relied on a tight timetable and when, on 31 July 1914, Russia decreed general mobilisation, the six-week clock started ticking.

The crisis had burst on a startled Europe on 24 July with news of a delayed but stiff Austrian ultimatum the day before to Serbia after the assassination of the heir to the Austrian throne with suspected Serbian involvement, but escalated quickly. As the prospect of general war loomed, Britain and Belgium each twice asked France and Germany whether they

Europe 1914

Petrograd (St Petersburg)

Riga

Moscow

Vilna

Königsberg

RUSSIAN EMPIRE

Warsaw   Brest-Litovsk

Kiev

Budapest

ARY

Odessa

ROMANIA

Belgrade   Bucharest

SERBIA   BULGARIA

RO   Sofia

Black Sea

ANIA

Constantinople

GREECE   **OTTOMAN EMPIRE**

Athens

would respect Belgian neutrality. France confirmed that it would; Germany did not. When on 31 July Berlin declared a state of imminent war, first Holland and then Belgium decreed general mobilisation. Although Holland was able to remain neutral, Belgium's precaution contributed to its resistance, which exceeded most expectations.

The Belgian Cabinet, however, cautiously did nothing and awaited events, which arrived quickly. On 2 August, Germany occupied Luxembourg and closed its border near Liège (Luik). That afternoon Hymans was made a Minister of State, entitled to attend Crown Councils. At 7:00 p.m. the German envoy presented a 12-hour ultimatum, demanding free passage for German troops. The Cabinet met at the palace and then with the Crown Council. Hymans was not the only Liberal member of the latter, but he was the only one in Brussels just then. Emile Vandervelde, leader of the Socialists, was also away and was made a Minister of State on 4 August as Belgium closed ranks and ensured that all voices were heard.

Emile Vandervelde (1866–1938) was a sociologist, author, professor at the Free University of Brussels, deputy, Socialist statesman and first President of the Second International, 1900–18. He engaged in missions to the United States in 1914, to Russia in 1917, and to Italy in 1918. As the first European socialist to join a Cabinet with party permission, he became Minister without Portfolio in 1916, of Procurement in 1917, of Justice in 1918–21, of Foreign Affairs in 1925–7, without Portfolio in 1935–6 and of Public Safety in 1936–7. He was also a member of the Belgian Academy. (See *The Democratic Socialism of Emile Vandervelde* by Janet Polasky.)

At the 2 August Crown Council, Hymans spoke forcefully for rejection of the ultimatum, which was agreed unanimously. He was appointed to a drafting committee of three. When it returned with a document to which each had contributed key sentences, the meeting approved it without discussion. At 7:00 a.m. on 3 August, the

Belgian rejection was handed to the German Minister. Only then did Belgium inform Britain, France and Russia of what had occurred. In view of recent events, there was no need to report to Austria, the other Guarantor Power, which in fact did not declare war on Belgium until 28 August. Belgium decided not to request aid until its frontier was breached.

That occurred on a large scale on 4 August, along with a German declaration of war. Thereupon Belgium requested aid from the three faithful Guarantors, saying it would defend itself. The interest of France, on whom Germany had already declared war, in aiding Belgium was obvious; Russia's support could be only nominal. Thus Britain was the key power. In debates during the previous week, its Cabinet had been unsure of the extent of its legal obligation, and ultimately made the decision as a matter of policy, though the defence of Belgium was emphasised to Parliament and the public. The issues were the existing European balance of power and whether Germany's effort to dominate the Continent would destroy that. These were matters of vital concern to Britain, as was ensuring that no Great Power dominated the Low Countries. The violation of Belgium and of the 1839 Treaties gave the Allies a much-needed cause regarding the sanctity of treaties and the rights of small states, especially after the German Chancellor deplored Britain's declaration of war over 'a scrap of paper'.[1] But he admitted to the Reichstag that Germany had wronged Belgium and promised post-war restoration. Nonetheless, many Britons, including some powerful ones, came to blame Belgium for Britain's involvement in the war, a factor which affected post-war policy.

Meanwhile, on 4 August a million German troops – an unprecedented number in military history to date – streamed across the border. At full mobilisation, Belgium could muster 265,000. Its heavily fortified strongholds were Liège, Antwerp and Namur (Namen). Of these, Liège with its 12 bridges across the Meuse was the gateway to Belgium. The city soon fell, but some of the 12 forts ringing it held out until 16 August, delaying the German advance. Brussels, which was not defensible, fell on 20 August. By then the King, Cabinet, officials and Crown Counsellors had withdrawn to Antwerp. The army did as well; from there it attacked the German flank, weakening its thrust into France, and tied up German forces while awaiting British aid. Flemings and Walloons alike wholeheartedly supported resistance; pre-war German popularity in Belgium had evaporated overnight. An exodus of civilian refugees to Holland, France and Britain began, soon encompassing nearly a quarter of the population of 7.5 million. Some later returned, some enlisted in the Belgian army and some remained abroad. The German army bypassed Antwerp and turned south. Namur, the last Belgian city on the Meuse Valley route into France, fell on 25 August. Three of Germany's six weeks had passed.

By then the head of government (*chef de cabinet*) Baron (later Count) Charles de Broqueville had decided to send a mission to the United States. He chose Hymans, Vandervelde, two Catholics and his own secretary who, like Hymans, was fluent in English. They left on 30 August via London where they received much praise and support. When they arrived in New York, they learned Germany had been halted at the Marne. They saw President Woodrow Wilson who was cordial but carefully neutral. During a propaganda tour ranging from George Washington's grave at Mount Vernon to Chicago, Montreal and points between, they prepared a book entitled *The Case of Belgium in the Present War*. Hymans wrote articles for the press. The trip accomplished nothing concrete, but possibly sowed seeds toward inclusion of Belgium in Wilson's later Fourteen Points.

By the time they returned in October, Antwerp had been abandoned, and the government was at Ostend on the coast. They arrived in time to be evacuated with the Cabinet to Le Havre in France. While Albert led his army along the coast to the Yser river, escaping German encirclement, the Belgian Cabinet in Exile established itself in the seaside resort suburb of Sainte-Adresse which became an extraterritorial enclave. Ministries occupied vacation villas vacant for the duration of the war, as did the Allied diplomatic corps. Cabinet meetings were held there or at the King's villa in La Panne (De Panne) in Belgium's 'little corner never conquered'.

In Sainte-Adresse, ministers accustomed to running large departments did not have much to do. Hymans undertook a mission to Holland and then attended academic conferences in France and wrote articles about Belgium as well as making visits to refugee centres, hospitals, conscripts and the trenches. Others did the same, but with so much time on their hands they bickered incessantly. They also became extremely well acquainted, a fact of importance in post-war politics. Hymans and Vandervelde had long known each other, but conservative Catholics who feared terrifying Marxists learned that the mild Vandervelde was another upper bourgeois Brussels intellectual. This eased his entry into post-war coalitions.

Tensions within the Cabinet were exacerbated by its disagreements with the King. The Cabinet was wholeheartedly with the Allies; Albert was not. His primary concerns were sparing his troops death, and the towns and countryside of Belgium devastation. He was deeply pessimistic, did not expect an Allied victory, and both anticipated and wanted a compromise peace. He long refused to put his army under

Allied command and rejected offensives he deemed hopeless. When the fall of Antwerp was imminent, he wished to surrender and was dissuaded only with great difficulty. Later in the war, he became embroiled in peace feelers, generally without the Cabinet's knowledge.[2] This conflicted with his public image as the heroic, handsome young King (39 years old in 1914) fighting on in Flanders Field and as the greatest of Belgium's three national symbols of resistance. Of the other two, Burgomaster Max's lack of subservience put him in a German prison for most of the war whereas Cardinal Désiré Mercier, Archbishop of Malines (Mechelen) and Primate of Belgium, an ardent patriot despite his disdain for the Flemings, nearly suffered the same fate after his pastoral letter at Christmas 1914.

If the Belgian government was wholeheartedly with the Allies, it was not of them. On this point, the Cabinet was agreed, as were the Allies. The Cabinet decided Belgium was a belligerent but not part of the Entente. Its special status might yield advantages though it was unclear whether neutrality and the 1839 Treaty system remained in effect. Belgium was not invited to adhere to the Declaration of London of 5 September 1914 whereby Britain, France and Russia agreed not to make a separate peace. Supposedly, Belgium's special status prevented adherence, but the fact that it was a small state probably mattered more. In any event, it did not ask to join but in the first year of the war worked to improve its ties with the three Great Powers and to promote its cause in friendly nations.

Meanwhile warfare in Belgium continued. The Battle of the Yser took place from 18 to 30 October 1914, roughly simultaneously with the First Battle of Ypres (Ieper). At the Yser, the Belgian army, with French and British support, held off the Germany army until the sluices at Nieuport (Nieuw-poort) were opened, flooding the area and forcing German forces to turn south to Ypres. There, where Adolf Hitler first saw action,[3] British, Indian, and Belgian troops fought the last battle of the race to the sea, suffering heavy losses. They held, saving the Channel ports needed for Allied resupply. The war of movement now ended, as did any major role for the Belgian army until nearly four years later, for the Second and Third Battles of Ypres mainly involved British forces. Deadly clashes occurred, but mostly the Belgian army sat and suffered in soggy trenches behind the Yser. The troops, always more Flemish than Walloon, were now about 80 per cent Flemings whereas their francophone officers did not speak their language, a factor contributing both to wartime German efforts to change Flemish loyalties and post-war Belgian reforms. Other forms of resistance included a vigorous clandestine press in occupied Belgium, most notably *De Vlaamische Leeuw* ('The Flemish Lion') and the impudent *La Libre Belgique* ('Free Belgium'), whose appearance was 'regularly irregular'[4] but which unfailingly arrived on the desk of the German Governor-General.

During the fighting in 1914, Belgium was constantly in the headlines of the world's press. There was a flood of praise for 'brave little Belgium' from editors and statesmen alike. As Belgium became the symbol of small states, British and French leaders provided frequent oratorical promises, often prefaced by 'I give you my word of honour', that they would fight on until Belgium was free and fully compensated. This was a heady diet for the leaders of a small state which had been far from the diplomatic mainstream, and they became addicted. As fighting moved elsewhere in 1915 and thereafter, oratory shifted to other battles and nations, but not without Belgian diplomats being instructed to insist upon it being mentioned. For the Allies, this became a nuisance. Moreover, Belgian leaders by and large believed the promises given to them. Doubting the word of honour of statesmen of the faithful Guarantor Powers was akin to doubting one's parents. In their inexperience of Great Power diplomacy, they did not realise that oratorical promises meant much less than written commitments. And as the war lengthened and broadened, they did not understand that after victory, if that arrived, they would be competing with other states, including Great Powers, for reconstruction funds.

German atrocities kept Belgium in the headlines and evoked sympathy through much of the war, but especially in 1914 and 1915. These were exaggerated by British wartime propaganda, and while no Belgian nuns were raped, outrages did occur but were excessively dismissed in the interwar era. Because the German army had been bedeviled in 1870 by French civilian guerrilla snipers (*francs-tireurs*), their troops were warned to expect them in Belgium and imbued with the myth of a Belgian People's War led by the clergy. In fact the Belgian Cabinet and local authorities, not wanting to give Germany any pretext, consistently urged calm and obedience. Aside from a few small scattered incidents, they were heeded, and 'atrocities' supposedly committed by Belgian civilians were imaginary. What frightened German troops thought were snipers, were usually German units or occasionally small stray Belgian troop detachments. The three-day sack of Louvain (Leuven), destroying the heart of a handsome medieval town and its great university library, was only the most famous and well-documented instance of arson, pillage and summary executions. Civilians were taken as hostages, used as human shields and deported to

Germany. Requisitions were severe, and forced financial contributions amounted to at least £100 million ($500 million), despite the 1907 Hague Convention on Land Warfare, to which Germany was a party.

Yet another matter evoking sympathy, especially in the United States, was the question of feeding the country, which normally imported 75 per cent of its calories. The British blockade, which included food, contributed to the problem and gave Germany a partial excuse, but the chief difficulty was the German refusal to feed its occupied territories. However, Belgium was free to solve the problem, which it did with the aid of the United States and other neutrals. Despite British objections based on fear that Germany would seize anything sent to Belgium, a system was in place by the end of October 1914. A Belgian National Committee of Relief and Alimentation and an American Commission for Relief in Belgium (CRB), the former dominated by Émile Francqui, director of Belgium's largest corporation, the Société Générale, the latter led by the engineer and future US President Herbert Hoover, already in London to rescue stranded Americans, worked well together as the two men had known each other in China. The Belgian Cabinet provided funds (largely borrowed) to buy food and other essentials in America; Hoover shipped these to Brand Whitlock, United States Minister in Brussels; and the Belgian Committee distributed and sold the food, using the funds received to pay government debts within Belgium. The Dutch and Spanish ministers joined in, creating a trio of 'protecting ministers'. When the United States became a belligerent in 1917, the other two continued the process. Britain created periodic difficulties, but its need for American funds and arms ensured that the flow was not impeded.

Amid sympathy for Belgium in the Western World, its

Foreign Ministry started considering the post-war peace settlement while still in Antwerp, but no decisions were taken.
Early efforts concerned its African colony. At first, Belgium
tried to neutralise the entire Congo Basin, but the Allies
did not agree. Then it tried to preserve the neutrality of the
Belgian Congo, also without Allied agreement. The matter
was settled when German gunboats on Lake Tanganyika
sank some Belgian vessels. Thereafter Belgian forces from the
Congo aided the Allies in conquering the Cameroons (Cam-
eroon) and came to the relief of the British at Abercorn (now
Mbata) in Northern Rhodesia (now Zambia). More importantly, Belgian African troops played a key role in 1916 in
German East Africa (Tanzania), seizing Ruanda (Rwanda),
Urundi (Burundi), and considerably more territory, including Tabora. This posed a dilemma for Britain which wanted
the entire colony but lacked the troops to conquer it without
substantial Belgian help. In time, Belgium ceded some areas,
including Tabora, but retained control of Ruanda and Urundi
for trading purposes. Its hope was that Britain would arrange
for Belgium to receive Cabinda and other Portuguese coastal
territory to widen the Congo's tiny Atlantic coastline, would
compensate Portugal elsewhere and would receive Ruanda
and Urundi for its efforts. Belgian leaders were utterly frank
about their aims, revealing their hand and gaining nothing
in return.

As Belgium's role in European battles dwindled, its leaders
contemplated the future. Oddly, one crucial matter was never
discussed. The Cabinet and senior officials so completely
agreed on full restitution of removals (ranging from art works
and agricultural implements, freight cars and other rolling
stock to entire factories, cattle to the cash deposit of the
National Bank); replacement where restitution was impossible,

as with burnt manuscripts and incunabula at Louvain; and compensation to the last franc for reconstruction expenses that debate seemed unnecessary. After all, the German Chancellor had promised this, and the faithful Guarantor Powers had sworn repeatedly to see to it. In their excessive faith in the value of Belgium's special position and in oral promises, it apparently never occurred to them that they would face stiff competition for Germany's finite resources. In the spring of 1915, they naively supposed that if Germany could not pay, the Allies would aid their country's reconstruction.

By then, Hymans had become Belgian Minister to Great Britain. He arrived in March 1915, remaining until October 1917, and became an admirer of the Foreign Secretary Sir Edward Grey. When he and Vandervelde joined the Cabinet in January 1916 as Ministers without Portfolio, he travelled monthly to Sainte-Adresse or La Panne for Cabinet meetings. In London he became thoroughly anglicised and thereafter was consistently anglophile. His reputation as a francophile rested on the results of British policy, shoving Belgium toward France, not on his preferences. While Belgian envoy, he worked on the feeding of Belgium and an abortive scheme to allow Belgian import of raw material and export of finished goods to alleviate an unemployment rate of 50 per cent. Also abortive was his effort to gain Belgian post-war inclusion in the British Empire's Imperial Preference trade system.

In London, Hymans worried about whether Belgium would be allowed to participate in peace negotiations, as did the Cabinet. In fact, the chief (but not the only) impediment to a negotiated peace was German insistence on gaining Belgian territory. Learning Allied decisions was difficult, however, and Belgium was not invited to Allied conferences. It seemed wise to ensure participation. The result was the

Declaration of Sainte-Adresse of 14 February 1916. It was drafted by the Belgian Foreign Ministry but, at French request, Britain deleted a reference to Belgium's 'just claims'. London and Paris issued the statement with Russia (plus Italian and Japanese consent) partly from concern over Albert's attitude and signs of discouragement in occupied Belgium. In April 1916, at Albert's insistence, the Declaration was extended to the Congo. These two Declarations were the most concrete achievements of Belgian wartime diplomacy.

The concern over participation arose during the Cabinet's initial contemplation of its aims. King and Cabinet agreed they wanted no part of wider Allied war aims; their goal was to defend and liberate Belgian soil. Beyond that was the question of Belgium's future international status. Views were mixed at first, but by early 1916 the newly reconstructed Cabinet unanimously favoured making neutrality optional; the King did not but bowed to the united front. As far as could be ascertained, occupied Belgium agreed with the Cabinet. Its replies in January and December 1917 to efforts for a compromise peace by Wilson and Pope Benedict XV respectively sought the territorial integrity of Belgium and the Congo, full political, economic and military independence, reparations and war costs and undefined guarantees and securities against future aggression. Only the last was controversial, as were unenunciated aims. Belgium was seeking to be independent but protected, to have its cake while eating it.

DECLARATION OF SAINTE-ADRESSE
'The Allied Guarantor Powers declare that, when the moment comes, the Belgian government will be called to participate in the peace negotiations and that they will not put an end to the hostilities unless Belgium is reestablished in its political and economic independence and largely indemnified for the damages which she has undergone. They will lend their aid to Belgium to assure her commercial and financial rehabilitation.'[5]

In their inexperience, its leaders did not see that in international politics, to get something one must give something, and Belgium had little to give. In mid-1916, as a substitute for obligatory neutrality it sought a guarantee from Britain and later France as well as Russia and Italy, offering nothing except self-defence but arguing that Belgium was essential to Anglo-French safety. Britain proposed a close military agreement, but after 80 years of neutrality Belgian aversion to alliances was so acute that the Cabinet and King instinctively rejected what Belgium's post-war diplomacy long sought.

Belgium also wanted true economic independence, having been under excessive German economic influence before the war. This would involve renegotiation of the Scheldt regime and, as was vainly hoped, perhaps an arrangement with Britain whose free trade tendencies Belgium shared but, more immediately, avoiding the customs union France periodically sought. In addition, there was concern about French tariffs and its surtax on overseas goods entering France via a non-French port, which had been a pre-war problem for Antwerp. If conceivably this surtax were imposed on entry into Alsace-Lorraine, Luxembourg and perhaps the Rhineland, the economic difficulties would multiply. Intermittent wartime negotiations achieved no resolution.

Through interminable debates, Belgian leaders reached a good deal of consensus on specific issues. On Belgium's list of priorities, neutrality was followed by reparations and then Luxembourg. This last was delicate since the Grand Duchy's status was similar, if not identical, to that of Belgium. It had become independent in 1890 when Queen Wilhelmina ascended the Dutch throne, passing to another branch of the German Nassau family. When that male line became extinct in 1912, the autocratic Marie Adelaide became Grand Duchess.

Her wartime policies favoured Germany, whereas her subjects did not, and the Allies expected both she and the dynasty would disappear at the war's end. So would the Duchy's membership in Germany's customs union and German control of its railways, which were short but strategic links on key main lines, including one from the Ruhr basin into France. Clearly, the tiny state (999 square miles, 2,587km^2) had to adhere, at least economically, to some neighbour. Belgium contemplated annexation, a personal dynastic union or economic union. Documents about the first two of these carried two conditions: if the Nassau dynasty ended or Luxembourg were not independent, and if the Luxembourgeois wanted to join Belgium. These were largely pro forma, as officials thought sentiment in Luxembourg favoured a Belgian solution, not realising that its anthem, which proclaimed 'we wish to remain what we are',[6] expressed the national attitude. In June 1917, the Belgian envoy in Paris gained from the French Premier Alexandre Ribot an oral statement, of which he was permitted to make formal written note, that France would not seek to annex Luxembourg. But a considerable propaganda campaign to that end existed in Paris, and thereafter France could not be moved a millimetre beyond Ribot's declaration.

In trying to shift Belgian attention in other directions, Paris often urged Belgium to claim the so-called 'Walloon Cantons', small border districts annexed by Prussia in 1915. The Cabinet was frankly interested in francophone Malmédy but undecided about the others. Occasionally, but especially in 1915, France also talked of Belgian annexation of the northern part of the Rhineland, with France to take the rest, or variously of an independent neutral buffer state. There was little official sentiment for annexation, but Belgium would have favoured the buffer state if it were truly independent, a subject on which Hymans harboured some wartime illusions. However, a French-dominated Rhineland was likely and clearly to be resisted in terms of economic encirclement.

Such French efforts were part of a larger campaign to reduce post-war Belgium to a political and economic satellite. Hence its pressure toward a customs union, its urging of claims on Germany, and especially its insistence that Belgium should seek Dutch territory. When Belgium resisted subservience, as it invariably did, French enthusiasm for Belgian aggrandisement evaporated, only to return when a new attempt was made. Constant French urging that Belgium air its claims to the Allies finally led to an approach to London, which refused discussion of them. This pattern repeated itself, with Britain very reserved about anything touching Holland, France equally reserved about Luxembourg and Britain refusing discussion of Belgium's now fully revealed desiderata until after the war.

Beyond modest claims on Germany, Belgium's territorial ambitions entailed two difficulties. Not only did they focus on neutral neighbours, but they were controversial among Belgian officialdom and opinion. A majority of Belgians seemed indifferent, preoccupied with the extreme difficulty of daily life. A small but vocal non-governmental element was intensely annexationist, seeking 'la grande Belgique' (large Belgium) and in some instances preoccupied with a revival of the 9th-century post-Charlemagne Middle Kingdom. This group pointed out that Belgium's 1839 truncation at all three corners had seriously impeded its defence and that the peace negotiations offered a unique opportunity to remedy the situation. Other annexationists were more moderate. Socialists and Flemings generally opposed annexations, as did Cardinal Mercier and adherents of 'little Belgium'. Some Catholics were hostile, whereas some in other parties worried about acquiring too many conservative Catholic voters. Several key Foreign Ministry officials were annexationist. Hymans initially was not, but, after a brief stint as Minister of Economic Affairs, he became Foreign Minister on 1 January 1918 in the last wartime Cabinet, and gradually absorbed Ministry views.

One 1839 truncation was Luxembourg; the other two were Flemish Zeeland and Limburg, both Dutch territory. The former had been neglected by the Dutch and its economic ties were to Belgium, but it had shown no interest in becoming Belgian. After hostilities ended, Queen Wilhelmina toured the area and promised reforms. Dutch Limburg, which jutted southward between Belgium and Germany and controlled the Meuse, on the other hand, had been part of Belgium from 1830 to 1839 and sympathised strongly with wartime Belgium. But it was the political stronghold of the Catholic party dominating the coalition installed in September 1918. Beyond territorial questions was that of the regime of the Scheldt, which flowed through 40 miles (64km) of Dutch territory to Belgium's main port of Antwerp. Since Holland saw no reason to benefit Antwerp at Rotterdam's expense, it had often made difficulties about dredging, pilotage and the like. On these questions, if not territorial ones, Britain offered some grounds for optimism.

The Cabinet at Sainte-Adresse was divided over territorial claims on Holland which, it assumed, would be compensated with nearby German districts. As Hymans said, good relations with Holland were important. In addition, though many refugees had returned home, 200,000 remained there. In 1916, a strident annexationist campaign for Luxembourg, Limburg, and Flemish Zeeland in the Belgian exile press led to a Dutch inquiry. The Allies disavowed the campaign, and the Belgian Foreign Minister at the time, Baron Napoleon Beyens, explicitly denied annexationist aims to the Dutch. As a consequence, Belgium never made any formal claim on Dutch territory, but disagreement over what to do continued at Sainte-Adresse and affected planning as the war neared its end. As Hymans gradually became more annexationist in mid-1918, he ultimately adopted the tactic of pointing to the drawbacks of the existing borders without making explicit claims – and hoping.

Early 1918 brought one final advantage to Belgium. Its efforts focused mostly on the faithful Guarantor Powers, but a new mission was sent to Washington after the United States entered the war in 1917. Perhaps its efforts contributed toward inclusion of Belgium in Wilson's Fourteen Points of 8 January 1918, summarising his peace programme. Because the armistice was, at German request, based on the Fourteen Points, inclusion of Belgium mattered, particularly since they implied the end of obligatory neutrality. Yet the statement partook of the oratorical vagueness of so many others (see Point VII in the panel overleaf).

In July 1918 the German advance was stopped, and soon Allied armies began to move eastward. The pace of Belgian diplomacy quickened, seeking British support and French concessions. King Albert was twice deployed to London, and Hymans sent a memorandum to the four main Allied Powers (now including Italy and the United States but not revolutionary Russia) formally announcing Belgium's renunciation of permanent neutrality and adding: *Moreover, it reserves to seek additional guarantees… . The circumstances in which peace is concluded will guide it in its claims.*[7] In fact, Belgian policy was now set on full revision of the 1839 Treaties, with all that might imply. By late September, the Belgian army, led

PRESIDENT WILSON'S FOURTEEN POINTS, 8 JANUARY 1918

The program of the world's peace, therefore, is our program; and that program, the only possible program, as we see it, is this:

I. Open covenants of peace, openly arrived at, after which there shall be no private international understandings of any kind but diplomacy shall proceed always frankly and in the public view.

II. Absolute freedom of navigation upon the seas, outside territorial waters, alike in peace and in war, except as the seas may be closed in whole or in part by international action for the enforcement of international covenants.

III. The removal, so far as possible, of all economic barriers and the establishment of an equality of trade conditions among all the nations consenting to the peace and associating themselves for its maintenance.

IV. Adequate guarantees given and taken that national armaments will be reduced to the lowest point consistent with domestic safety.

V. A free, open-minded, and absolutely impartial adjustment of all colonial claims, based upon a strict observance of the principle that in determining all such questions of sovereignty the interests of the populations concerned must have equal weight with the equitable claims of the government whose title is to be determined.

VI. The evacuation of all Russian territory and such a settlement of all questions affecting Russia as will secure the best and freest cooperation of the other nations of the world in obtaining for her an unhampered and unembarrassed opportunity for the independent determination of her own political development and national policy and assure her of a sincere welcome into the society of free nations under institutions of her own choosing; and, more than a welcome, assistance also of every kind that she may need and may herself desire. The treatment accorded Russia by her sister nations in the months to come will be the acid test of their good will, of their comprehension of her needs as distinguished from their own interests, and of their intelligent and unselfish sympathy.

VII. Belgium, the whole world will agree, must be evacuated and restored, without any attempt to limit the sovereignty which she enjoys in common with all other free nations. No other single act will serve as this will serve to restore confidence among the nations in the laws which they have themselves set and determined for the government of their relations with one another. Without this healing act the whole structure and validity of international law is forever impaired.

VIII. All French territory should be freed and the invaded portions restored, and the wrong done to France by Prussia in 1871 in the matter of Alsace-Lorraine, which has unsettled the peace of the world for nearly fifty years, should be righted, in order that peace may once more be made secure in the interest of all.

IX. A readjustment of the frontiers of Italy should be effected along clearly recognizable lines of nationality.

X. The peoples of Austria-Hungary, whose place among the nations we wish to see safeguarded and assured, should be accorded the freest opportunity to autonomous development.

XI. Rumania, Serbia, and Montenegro should be evacuated; occupied territories restored; Serbia accorded free and secure access to the sea; and the relations of the several Balkan states to one another determined by friendly counsel along historically established lines of allegiance and nationality; and international guarantees of the political and economic independence and territorial integrity of the several Balkan states should be entered into.

XII. The Turkish portion of the present Ottoman Empire should be assured a secure sovereignty, but the other nationalities which are now under Turkish rule should be assured an undoubted security of life and an absolutely unmolested opportunity of autonomous development, and the Dardanelles should be permanently opened as a free passage to the ships and commerce of all nations under international guarantees.

XIII. An independent Polish state should be erected which should include the territories inhabited by indisputably Polish populations, which should be assured a free and secure access to the sea, and whose political and economic independence and territorial integrity should be guaranteed by international covenant.

XIV. A general association of nations must be formed under specific covenants for the purpose of affording mutual guarantees of political independence and territorial integrity to great and small states alike.

by King Albert but under the ultimate command of the Allied Supreme Commander Marshal Ferdinand Foch, began the liberation of Belgium. By early October the royal family was at Bruges (Brugge). Meanwhile, Hymans had laid out Belgian conditions for an armistice, including Belgian participation in any military occupation of Luxembourg. These were sent to the Allies, along with the first of many futile requests that Belgium be the seat of the Peace Conference ahead. Seeking this honour was a domestic political necessity, but Hymans, who claimed in his memoirs that he did not anticipate success, pursued it excessively and became a nuisance.

In mid-October Hymans was one of many persons from Sainte-Adresse and occupied Belgium who consulted with the King on the creation of a new three-party Cabinet to replace the existing ministry when the King reached Brussels and a programme of reforms to be announced then, for there was concern about revolution or difficulties with ardent support-ers of the Flemish cause. Albert chose as his chief minister Leon Delacroix, a Catholic political novice not associated with past quarrels who had stayed in Brussels through the war. On the advice of Hymans, who was to remain Foreign Minister, the title of *chef de cabinet* was abandoned in favour of that of Prime Minister.

Hymans then made his first visit to Paris since becoming Foreign Minister. On 23 and 24 October he saw his coun-terpart Stephen Pichon, Prime Minister Georges Clem-enceau and President Raymond Poincaré, all of whom were extremely reserved about Luxembourg. Although alteration of Dutch frontiers did not look promising, France supported modification of the Scheldt regime and Belgian acquisition of the Walloon Cantons. French leaders pressed for a close rela-tionship, including a customs union and a military accord.

Though Hymans did not want a French accord without a concomitant British one, his assessment was rather optimistic. He thought France would either take Luxembourg or let Belgium have it on condition of a military accord.

Clemenceau told Hymans, as he knew from the press, that Germany had asked Wilson for an armistice, but not that Allied meetings to discuss terms would take place in Paris in a few days. On his return to Belgium, Hymans, who had already told Whitlock Belgium expected to be consulted as it had conditions, learned of these meetings and awaited an invitation which did not come. Belgian plaints finally produced a summons, but so late that much was already settled. Belgium gained only the evacuation of Luxembourg and immediate return of the reserves of the Belgian National Bank.

More political consultations with the King were followed by the armistice on 11 November and progressive liberation of Belgian territory. The King and new Cabinet returned to Brussels on 21 November, and Albert addressed the legislative chambers the next day. With questionable constitutionality but some urgency, he announced the agreed reforms: renunciation of obligatory neutrality, a new Flemish university at Ghent, reforms for the benefit of the working class, changes in the legal code, equal rights for both languages and an end to plural voting. Though these reforms were designed to provide genuine equality for all, votes for women, which Hymans favoured, was excluded as too divisive at a time when national unity was imperative.

At the Foreign Ministry, Hymans and his staff set about planning for the Peace Conference with startlingly little awareness of what lay ahead. Despite the difficulties over entry into the armistice talks, they did not foresee that Belgium's participation in the Peace Conference would be more nominal than substantive. The fact that much hard work had yielded few commitments did not alarm them. They were excessively optimistic and placed too much trust in the two faithful Guarantor Powers, stressing Belgium's strategic position, its similar military interests to France and its economic interests akin to Britain's. They did not see that both Great Powers would put their own interests first, nor that the precarious wartime Anglo-French partial unity was rapidly dissolving, which would frustrate Hymans' hope for close solidarity with both Powers. And, given their geographic location and past history, they did not examine the contradiction inherent in their aspiration toward full sovereignty, real security, and true independence.

The fact that most of the territories they wanted belonged to an ally (Portugal) or neutrals did not seem insuperable, and thinking was increasingly dominated by what seemed a unique opportunity to right the 'wrongs' of 1839. Belgian leaders relied with considerable naiveté on their impeccable moral and legal status, pointing out that only two small states had fought the war throughout, and that while Serbia's role in the war's onset was rather murky, theirs was not. Belgium's transcendent experience remained very important to them, and they did not realise that it was no longer so to others, nor that at Paris there would be 22 small states, not two. In short, neither their previous sheltered existence nor life at Sainte-Adresse had taught them the hard facts of international politics or the realities of power. An abrupt awakening lay ahead.

The Anglo Belgian Conference at Chequers. Paul Hymans (left) is photographed with Premier Ramsay Macdonald and Belgian Prime Minister Georges Theunis. The Assistant Under-Secretary of Foreign Affairs Sir Eyre Crowe stands behind the trio. 3rd May 1924.

II
The Paris Peace Conference

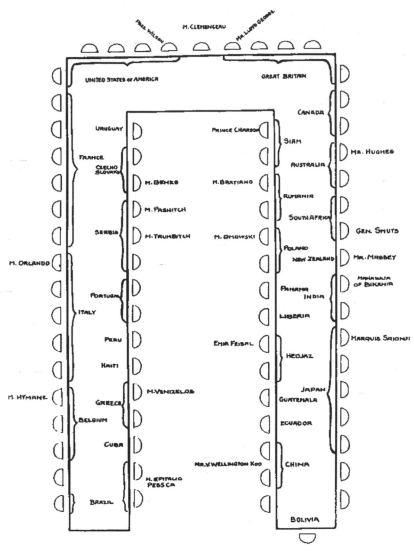

Sketch of the seating plan at the Paris Peace Conference.

4

Baptism by Total Immersion

In a sense, the Paris Peace Conference was Belgium's diplomatic debut, its true introduction to Great Power diplomacy. The country had not existed at the time of the Congress of Vienna and had attended few important gatherings since. Its leaders, especially Hymans, received an essential, intensive – if jarring – education where they suddenly had to acquire a new language and accept a new reality. For this they were unprepared, having believed promises of participation and countless expressions of gratitude for Belgian resistance having allegedly saved Europe in 1914. Hymans figuratively gasped for air and later said the Conference was the most painful period of his life, but it proved to be a key phase in Belgium's astoundingly rapid transition from the status of a sheltered child unaware of the ways of the international world, to that of the post-war hinge of the Western Entente.

Hymans and his staff prepared their dossiers and made their wishes known to the Allies, chiefly the two faithful Guarantor Powers. But they did not prepare the ground as fully as they might have, especially with the United States, for they did not foresee the struggle ahead. Equally, they remained unaware of Holland's measures to counter Belgium's hope for Dutch territory. Since unofficial signs indicated that Belgium would have three plenipotentiaries, one was chosen from each party. But the official invitation on 13 January specified only two. This was the doing of the British Prime Minister David Lloyd George, who was already turning against France and assumed Belgium was a French satellite. Furious Belgian protests ensued. Over British objections, a Great Power meeting awarded Belgium and Serbia each three plenipotentiaries. Thus the Belgian delegation arrived pleased and optimistic, unaware that only a domestic political problem had been solved.

Since Delacroix remained in Brussels to cope with reviving a country which had been picked clean, had an 80 per cent unemployment rate, and lacked anything to work with, Hymans led the delegation as its Liberal member. He also was entirely dominant, supported primarily by his Foreign Ministry staff. Hymans chose the Fleming Jules van den Heuvel as the Catholic member whereas Vandervelde chose himself as the Socialist, much to Hymans' annoyance.

Vandervelde played a double role tailored to public support of international socialism and his own party but private support of the delegation. As socialists opposed annexations, he did as well, though calling acquisition of the Walloon Cantons 'disannexation', a term he applied also to voluntary rapprochement with Luxembourg. He favoured reparations and revision of the Scheldt regime. At Paris, he went his own way, working on the Labour Charter and the founding of the International Labour Organisation, but standing with the delegation on all major occasions. There and in his memoirs, he blamed everything socialists disliked on Hymans and carefully built a paper record consonant with his role in international socialism, but in his private actions (and later as Foreign Minister) he was a Belgian nationalist.

Like Vandervelde, van den Heuvel opposed annexation of Dutch territory without consent; but along with Hymans, he was willing for the Conference to arrange transfer to Belgium with compensation to Holland from Germany. He was a professor, a distinguished jurist of international law, a former minister of justice and wartime envoy to the Vatican, as well as a Minister of State. He spoke well, with a certain Latin finesse. Lloyd George said: 'He argues like an Italian.'[1] He did good work in the Peace Conference Commission on Reparations, but decisions were not made there. For broader tasks, he was probably too old, too traditionalist, and too inclined to rest on a legal case. And his ties to the Vatican did not help with Clemenceau and Lloyd George.

Most of the burden rested on Hymans, who thought the Peace Conference was Belgium's big chance and became over-zealous, tending to nag to the point where he became known as 'that pestiferous mosquito Hymans'.[2] He was a good administrator, planned policy well, carried the Cabinet easily and usually spotted coming policies of neighbouring powers, though he sometimes rejected his instincts, especially as to Britain, refusing to face facts. He had a logical mind, elegance and full command of the diplomatic niceties. A Foreign Minister must usually be a nationalist, but Hymans was also an intense patriot; he was extremely sensitive to slights to Belgium, which caused him to flare up, sometimes explosively. He took the technical equality of sovereign states as reality, acting as an equal and saying that Belgium would not beg, when in fact it was doing so. To what extent he expected to gain Dutch territory is unclear; at the time, some held that he hinted at much in hopes of gaining a bit, responded to political and public pressure or worried about his party's future.

As a diplomat, Hymans was neither tactful nor agreeable in this first foray. He was too frank, with little humour and imagination because this opportunity mattered so much, and enraged those he needed to charm. He bored others in his hopeless quest for Brussels as the seat of the League of Nations (as Belgian opinion ardently desired) and in overly long speeches arising from his compulsion toward precision, his career as a legislator and his belief that a strong speech would prevail. He did not appreciate how others reacted to him, seemed unaware of the time pressures on the four leading statesmen – Clemenceau, Lloyd George, Orlando and Wilson – and made no effort to steer Belgian opinion toward a reality he had not faced. He remarked that the Big Four, as this quartet became known, thought *that it would be impertinent for the small states to claim to participate in the debates of the mighty*.[4] This he saw but did not yet accept. He cited wartime promises, insisted on Belgium's special rights, and remarked that failing to recognise them would be extraordinary ingratitude. As time passed without participation or access, he became a trifle frantic about losing Belgium's big chance – and tried harder. By May he learned the realities of power and realised his challenges had been costly – but by then the damage had been done.

It has been suggested that Belgium should have sent Beyens, a career diplomat, or the tactful de Broqueville.[5] That was not practical politics. Either might have gained more information and possibly a little more participation, but even the most

> 'When he [Hymans] dominated the conversation, he thought he dominated the situation.'
>
> DAVID LLOYD GEORGE[3]

skilled diplomat could not overcome Belgium's status as a small state, its lack of bargaining chips and the attitudes of its two faithful Guarantors. Nor could much be done about a deft Dutch campaign. After centuries of European statecraft, the Netherlands knew exactly how to treat Great Powers and was never a nuisance. As a neutral, Holland was not invited to the Conference, but it sent its best diplomats to the Paris legation to offer cash, credits, cows and reconstruction aid, all contingent upon French abandonment of support for Belgian claims on Holland. France could not do so altogether but kept its backing at an ineffectual level. In short, Hymans aggravated difficulties but created few.

The Belgian delegation soon realised that Conference plenary sessions were little more than formalities. At the second one on 25 January 1919, Clemenceau, as President of the Conference, announced the creation of five (later seven) Commissions, on which the five 'powers of general interests' would each have three seats and the 22 'powers of limited interests' would collectively have five seats. Hymans protested this disparity, followed by leaders of three other small states, Clemenceau abruptly declared that the millions of dead of the Great Powers entitled them to dominate. Hymans subsided, reflecting that sometimes *it is necessary to have the courage to be silent*[6] but rarely following his own advice.

Hymans wisely declined a Serbian request to lead a bloc of small states, but when their delegates met two days later to choose Commission members, by arrangement he stated their united complaints, sparing others who feared Clemenceau's revenge. By his outspokenness along with his oral and written protests, he became *de facto* spokesman of the small nations, gaining prominence at a price. Ultimately Belgium obtained one or sometimes two seats on all seven Commissions.

The smaller states viewed Belgium as a special case in that its legal status in the war was unique, it alone among them was participating in the Rhineland occupation, it was the only small state with large reparation claims on Germany and the only one concerned with Germany's western frontier. The Great Powers did not agree. Partly they feared setting a precedent. Partly it was too much trouble to summon Hymans, especially after the Big Four (or Council of Four) began meeting on 24 March, and its agenda hopped erratically from topic to topic. As crucial debates began in April, dislike of him or of Belgium's policy was a factor as well.

> The Great Powers are bullying the little States; they are not showing the proper respect for our national rights.
>
> PAUL HYMANS[7]

Belgian Commission members were able, hard-working and useful, but Commissions had no power of decision. Moreover, in the key Commission on Reparations, the British, French and American experts often huddled together privately. Belgium deemed the Commission on Ports, Waterways and Railways vital, and initially questions about the Scheldt were sent there but soon were shifted. Most importantly, as territorial Commissions were created, only delegates of the five Great Powers sat on them. No Belgian was a member of the Belgian (later Belgian and Danish) Commission.

The League of Nations Commission, on which Hymans sat, began work at once, meeting at night so as not to delay business. He annoyed members by talking too much, especially about Brussels as seat of the League, and was relegated with other loquacious members to a 'clarification' committee so the rest could proceed. Hymans infuriated the French by not supporting an entity with military means and outraged the British by demanding seats for small states on the League Council where originally only the five Great Powers would sit. When Britain finally conceded two seats for the smaller states, Hymans shouted: *What you propose is a revival of the Holy Alliance of unhallowed memory!*[8] Further protests gained the small states four seats, a signal victory but a costly one.

During the daytime at first, the Big Four and Japan were taking each other's measure on key issues, addressing secondary questions and postponing major battles. Among other matters, they informally allocated colonies. As this became known, Belgium sought a meeting with the Council of Ten, consisting of the two ranking delegates of the five Great Powers, usually the Prime Minister and Foreign Minister. On 30 January this was granted, and Belgium claimed Ruanda and Urundi. As Britain wanted all of German East Africa, there was no sequel but silence. This pattern repeated itself often. Then the Ten took on a new task. As the 22 smaller states present had little to do, they needed the appearance of some activity for their domestic political survival. So each was awarded a hearing before the Ten, where most merely recited documents already submitted. Belgium was no exception.

Belgium's three-hour session fell on 11 February. All three plenipotentiaries attended, but Hymans alone spoke, seeking full revision of the 1839 Treaties, with all that might imply, particularly since he sought Belgian sovereignty over the western Scheldt and the Ghent-Terneuzen Canal. He described the drawbacks of the existing situation in peace and war but offered no solution. When asked how Dutch territory could be transferred without compensation, he mentioned adjoining German areas but said he was referring the problem to the Conference, which he hoped would join and support Belgium in negotiations with Holland. He noted

BELGIUM BEFORE THE COUNCIL OF TEN, 11 FEBRUARY 1919
M. Hymans: ...*The war had destroyed the foundations of Belgium's political status, and economically had ruined the country.*
The Belgians therefore asked the Allied and Associated Powers, at whose side they fought, and in particular the two Powers – signatories to and Guarantors of the Treaties of 1839 – to help them to set up a strong and prosperous Belgium, restored to full and complete political and economic sovereignty. This demand was in accord with the seventh point of President Wilson's Declaration to Congress on the 8th January 1918. The Belgians were asking the Great Powers to furnish them with the conditions of stability which might enable them to encounter new dangers. Belgium was at the sensitive point of Western Europe, protecting the coast of the North Sea, and consequently Great Britain and the Northern frontier of France. The security of Belgium was therefore in the hands of France and Great Britain and the interests of all three Powers were bound up together.

In concluding, M. Hymans said that he wished to observe that *the Treaties of 1815, 1831, and 1839 had also served Prussian policy in its thrust toward the Meuse. He hoped he had succeeded in convincing the meeting that these treaties must be revised and that the Belgian claims were legitimate. Belgium had demanded no guarantees when she took up arms. She had done her whole duty, but she had suffered grievously and was still suffering. Her industry was ruined and could not revive for many months. Belgium was not asking for the price of her services, and was animated by no spirit of conquest or imperialist ambitions. All Belgium asked from the Great Allied and Associated Powers was the conditions necessary to ensure the future and prosperity of the country.*[9]

Belgium's wish for rapprochement with Luxembourg, preferably political union. Very briefly, he mentioned interest in the Walloon Cantons, notably Malmédy, and the tiny border territory of Moresnet (now la Calamine, Kelmis or Kalmis). He sought full sovereignty for Belgium and participation in discussions of the Rhineland.

The next day the British Foreign Secretary, Arthur Balfour, gave the Ten a draft for a five-Power Belgian Commission to advise about the transfer of Malmédy, the incorporation of Moresnet and the possible transfer of German territory to Holland in relation to Belgian claims for sovereignty on the Scheldt and in southern Limburg. This was approved without discussion. The resulting Commission was chaired by Clemenceau's confidant, André Tardieu, who was friendly to Belgium, as was the Harvard historian Charles Homer Haskins. The other key members were Sir Eyre Crowe and Sir James Headlam-Morley, both of the Foreign Office. Crowe was less hostile to Belgium than other senior Foreign Office officials but rarely supported its claims; Headlam-Morley was more sympathetic but more junior. Tardieu soon gained a mandate to present proposals on all aspects of revision of the 1839 Treaties, including in his eyes the Scheldt regime and that of the Ghent-Terneuzen Canal. At Balfour's instance, however, the Commission was not to deal with Luxembourg. It was, he said, a purely political question not requiring commission work, and reserved to the Five, soon to become the Big Four, since Japan's interests in German and League questions had already been addressed.

Hymans followed his appearance with a formal request for attendance at sessions where questions of interest to Belgium were discussed, and gained written assurances of participation in German questions. Partly in reaction to French pressure, he made futile efforts to see Lloyd George (whose hostility predated any acquaintance), even rashly addressing one request *from one first delegate to another first delegate.*[10] He would have been wiser to focus on the American delegation which, unlike the other two, had no axes to grind. Haskins was friendly, as was Wilson, who consented to visit Belgium but no other small state. The Secretary of State Robert Lansing was cool, but he had little influence except on Belgian-Dutch negotiations. Most important was Wilson's confidant, Colonel Edward M House (an honorary Texas colonel, not a military man) who proved to be Belgium's best friend at the Conference.

France pushed Hymans, who still thought mainly of faithful Guarantors, toward the Americans, but otherwise presented problems. Heavy pressure was exerted toward a sweeping political, economic and military scheme rendering Belgium a satellite and, in French eyes, the battleground in the next war. As Hymans did not oblige, France sought payment of a loan and recognition of its war debt with five per cent interest, though Belgium visibly could not pay at present. Clemenceau assured Hymans that France would not annex Luxembourg, but he clearly meant to dominate it, or at least its railways, and wanted Belgian support for a long occupation of the Rhineland.

On the other hand, Lloyd George already deemed France too strong and Belgium its satellite. His desire that Germany balance France was bolstered by fear that it would refuse to sign the Treaty or become Bolshevik. He knew Belgium was an economic rival of Scotland, where Belgian cast iron undersold the domestic product on the Glasgow market. Moreover, it was the only small state with a large claim on German reparations, potentially reducing the British share. And a misaddressed envelope revealed to Hymans that Britain rejected any scheme to give Belgium Dutch territory with compensation from Germany, or any change of sovereignty on the Scheldt, out of fear of submarines. Belgium found itself caught between France's security concerns and Britain's misreading of the power balance, and so it remained for years. Neither desired Belgian participation, and creation of the Council of Four doomed its hope of systematic attendance.

Some of the difficulties appeared when Hymans was suddenly summoned on short notice to meet with the new Council of Four on 31 March. He understood the topic was the Walloon Cantons but intentionally broadened the discussion, saying: *If the left bank of the Rhine is to be occupied, Belgium will have to take part. We would not like to hear it said, some fine day, that the Great Powers came to this or that decision without consulting us.*[11] When he complained of lack of contact with the Four and support from the Great Powers in general, Lloyd George exploded, citing Australia's and Britain's war dead in Flanders. Hymans

'Remember, Your Majesty, that there has been only one great King in the past five hundred years.'
GEORGES CLEMENCEAU TO KING ALBERT[12]

expressed gratitude for wartime efforts and, along with Wilson, tried to soothe Lloyd George, but to no avail. He was not invited back.

The difficulties of access led Hymans to summon King Albert, for nobody could refuse to see the King of the Belgians. He made the rounds, receiving complaints from Clemenceau about the Belgian delegation in general and Hymans in particular, with claims that France would assume defence of Belgian rights. In a meeting with the Four on 4 April, Albert complained of lack of consultation and of learning about questions concerning Belgium from the newspapers. He gained assurances of consultation, but since he also opposed a long Rhineland occupation and France saw no virtue in adding to the number of its opponents, these promises were not honoured.

The Rhineland question was important to Belgium since it had been participating in the military occupation, holding the northernmost zone, from the armistice on. Moreover,

economic ties were close, and fears that France would dominate the entire Rhineland were great. There were Anglo-
American loans to consider as well. In its zone, Belgium
gained an unintended reputation for rigour, mainly because
it honoured Foch's directives until it learned that the Anglo-
Americans were ignoring them, and because Germans
especially resented the presence of a small nation. Belgium
favoured a demilitarised and neutral Rhineland but not a long
occupation. If such were to be, however, it would participate
in order to shrink the French zone and keep it away from
Belgian borders. Despite the agitation of a few super-patriots, Belgium had no aspirations to German territory beyond
Moresnet and the Walloon Cantons.

Hymans raised the question of participation in the Rhineland debates, which preoccupied the Four in late March and
much of April, repeatedly with the British and French, but
not with the Americans who might have been more accommodating. Italy, which was not to participate in the occupation, was present at the debates, and also sometimes Japan.
The matter was settled on 22 April, but Hymans was not told,
though the Powers took it for granted that Belgium, with the
second largest force in the Rhineland, would participate in
the ongoing occupation and the new Inter-Allied Rhineland
High Commission they created on 21 April. This disregard
was mostly a matter of habit and of the fact that Belgium's
role was an anomaly.

When the separatist Rhenish Republic, a creation of French
generals but not of Clemenceau, was declared on 1 June, the
Belgian military commander and government were confused
due to lack of information but cautious. They wished to
march with the Allies, assuming erroneously that Foch spoke
for them, but wisely sought confirmation from the Four. Since

they gained no information, they did not act, and the Republic was not proclaimed in the Belgian zone before its rapid collapse. In the next two weeks, the Powers debated the duration of the Rhineland occupation without informing or consulting Hymans. On 16 June Britain, France and the United States signed a Rhineland Agreement regarding the military occupation in the presence of Italy and Japan. Again, Hymans was neither consulted nor informed. Lloyd George told Sir Maurice Hankey to prepare a similar document for Belgium to sign, but this was not done. On 4 August, Hymans learned from the newspaper *Le Temps* of the existence of a Rhineland Declaration raising the possibility of early evacuation if Germany fulfilled the Treaty, particularly regarding reparations and disarmament, or provided guarantees that it would do so. As he protested, he received a copy of both the Declaration and the Rhineland Agreement but was not asked to sign either.

The Belgian struggle to participate in debates about German reparation payments for civilian damage followed the same pattern. Hymans realised French, British and Italian appetites were large and feared Belgium might get little. His attempts to join in the debates of the Four were futile, but they aroused the interest of House whose efforts yielded Belgium's most valuable gains at the Conference. Also, a crisis over Belgian reparations late on gained Belgium a seat (which became crucial after the United States withdrew) on the permanent Reparations Commission. This catapulted Belgium to the centre of post-war reparations diplomacy at the core of the continuing power struggle.

Meanwhile, the Belgian Commission was dealing with Belgium's claims on Germany and with Dutch questions without Belgian participation, which was also withheld on various lesser committees. By mid-April, Hymans had accepted the situation. He now concentrated on seeking to be informed of decisions affecting Belgium, but most of his information continued to come from the press. As the small states were to see the Treaty text only one day before the Germans, Hymans gained permission from Clemenceau to see it earlier, but without effect. On 1 May, six days before presentation to Germany, the Belgian delegation was obliged to ask the Four for clauses which had to be submitted to the King of the Belgians.

Belgium's continual difficulties of access arose from disdain for small states, dislike of Hymans, simple inconvenience, reluctance to acknowledge that Belgium's role regarding the German Treaty was unique among the lesser powers, and Lloyd George's hostility to Belgium. That hostility permeated much of the British delegation and affected many matters, including intangible ones. The social life of the Peace Conference was considerable, and other Great Powers accepted Hymans' invitations and invited him in return. From the British delegation only the economist John Maynard Keynes came to dine, and no invitations were received. Only one of Hymans' many letters to Lloyd George – offering the Egmont Palace for the League's seat – received a reply, a curt one-sentence acknowledgement from his secretary. After the Peace Conference, France renewed its effort to make Belgium a satellite, showering medals around, trying to buy the Brussels press, and sending senior dignitaries in a campaign unmatched by Britain, which seemed indifferent. In addition, in the first departure from the longstanding tradition that embassies were exchanged only among Great Powers whereas lesser states sent and received ministers at legations, France raised its Brussels legation to an embassy, forcing others to do the same. Britain did so only grudgingly and belatedly.

The greatest balm to the bruised Belgian national ego was probably Wilson's visit on 18 and 19 June. He dutifully made the appropriate rounds, said the United States would elevate its legation in recognition of Belgium's new status as an equal member of the family of nations and in a poignant ceremony befitting his former academic career was awarded an honorary Doctorate of Laws in the ruins of the library of Louvain. The special honour of the Presidential visit was well received amid almost universal Belgian dissatisfaction with the terms of the Versailles Treaty. Curiously, the dissatisfaction did not affect Hymans' standing, though Wilson came and went whereas the Treaty terms were there to stay.

> We have done our duty; we have had very bitter disappointments; we pursued a beautiful dream and, if we were not able to realise it, that is because the general political circumstances were not favourable for us and because we did not receive the support on which we counted. But in politics, one must distinguish what is possible from what is desirable.
>
> **PAUL HYMANS**[13]

All in all, Paul Hymans found the Peace Conference a painful and exhausting experience wherein he lost many illusions. With the responsibility on his shoulders, he fought fiercely but often to little effect through an initially bewildering struggle. He learned the hard way what participation meant for a small state, what the gratitude of which so much had been heard amounted to, and how Belgium's 'rights' were regarded by the Great Powers. He emerged in June a more experienced and effective diplomat than he had been in January.

5

Territorial Aspirations

The overriding difficulty with Belgian territorial ambition was that its most important desires entailed territory of allies, neighbours and neutrals. Hymans understood this and carefully avoided claims on Dutch, Luxembourgeois or Portuguese territory (though seeking Dutch waters), but his faith in the Great Powers was such that he thought something could be arranged. In addition, he and his colleagues misread the situation, anticipating British support regarding Holland and German East Africa but French help on Luxembourg, and thus revealed their hand to those who opposed them. Hymans apparently had not fully realised to what extent Belgium's goals clashed with the concerns of the faithful Guarantor Powers, on whom he relied too trustingly. They had the power and used it to decide according to their own interests. To a degree, Hymans saw this but did not accept it, having believed their protestations.

Hymans enjoyed one advantage early on when many territorial decisions were taken. Belgian opinion was distracted, and so was the Cabinet, by the misery of daily life and the catastrophic economic condition of the country, leaving the delegation relatively free except for pressure from the political extremes. The super-patriots of the Comité de Politique Nationale (CPN, Committee of National Policy), who were not numerous, agitated for maximum territorial gains. At the other end of the spectrum, the Socialist Party shrewdly opposed territorial solutions to Belgium's security problem. Vandervelde pursued his double role, supporting the massive Revendications Belges (Belgian Claims) submitted to the Belgian Commission at the end of February, though he reserved on territorial transfer if the population opposed it. After assurances from Hymans, the two men agreed that territorial transfer was acceptable if the Great Powers endorsed it.

The Belgian Commission worked quickly, starting with claims on Germany. The least of these addressed an historical anomaly. A drafting error in the Final Act of Vienna in 1815 divided the small town of Moresnet, leaving part in Holland (later Belgium), part (1.3 square miles or 3.37km²) in Prussia, and 1.21 square miles (3.13km²) to nobody. After 1816, this portion was jointly administered by both states. Its zinc mines had been worked out, but its forests were needed to replace indiscriminate wartime German felling in Belgium, and the stateless inhabitants who had petitioned for incorporation in Belgium in the past did so again. The Commission recommended unifying all three portions of Moresnet in Belgium with an accretion of 3,400 inhabitants, some of them German. This was approved, despite German protests.

Of the several Walloon Cantons on the Belgian-German border awarded to Prussia in 1815, Belgium sought Malmédy. It included the old Belgian Canton of St Vith, railways running to the border, and a large German military camp. With an area of 314 square miles (813.5km²) and a population of 37,000 which was 80 per cent Walloon (and had been 100 per cent Walloon until shortly before the war), it had been the main point of the German attack. Numerous residents petitioned to join Belgium. Again, the Commission endorsed transfer, although Headlam-Morley insisted the inhabitants should have a right of protest.

Hymans, who wished to incorporate as few Germans as possible, hesitated over the smaller Walloon Canton of Eupen (68 square miles or 176km² and 27,000 inhabitants) which was linguistically mixed but much more Germanic than Malmédy with correspondingly fewer petitions for incorporation in Belgium. Economic and electoral questions mattered, especially since gaining Dutch districts seemed questionable, but the decisive factor was the Belgian army's General Staff which wanted both cantons for a more defensible border. At the end of February 1919, in a hasty ill-considered decision, the Belgian delegation decided to seek Eupen, though Hymans asked for less territory than the army desired. In the Belgian Commission, France and Italy endorsed the Belgian request, the latter seeking to set precedents for its grandiose claims elsewhere, while the Anglo-Americans resisted. Japan, as usual, awaited a majority decision to accept. Ultimately, the British and Americans agreed to cession subject to a right of protest.

After the Four approved, both cantons were transferred to Belgian occupation. When the Versailles Treaty came into force on 10 January 1920, Belgium gained sovereignty over Moresnet, Malmédy and Eupen. Thus 63,000 inhabitants were transferred, not all of them German, though too many of them were, as Hymans feared, probably without improving Belgium's defensive line enough to matter. When Germany began its drive for territorial revision of the Treaty in 1925 and 1926, it aimed first at the weakest point on its borders and sought retrocession of Eupen and Malmédy, creating new crises. In the interim, however, Belgium gained one additional advantage. Unlike all other recipients of German territory except France, it was exempted from paying for German state properties in the ceded districts. It was not, however, excused from assuming a portion of the Second Reich's state debts as of 1 August 1914 and was obliged to pay 640,609 gold marks ($160,152 or £32,030) in regard to Eupen and Malmédy.

Immediately upon gaining sovereignty, Belgium opened the required protest registers. It scrupulously followed the Treaty terms, even opening the registers after church on Sunday to facilitate access. Departing German officials and railway workers had to show proof of protest to get new jobs in Germany. When the registers closed after six months, Eupen had recorded 218 protests out of 13,975 eligible voters, 121 from German officials. In Malmédy, there were 62 protests (four later withdrawn) out of 19,751 eligible voters, more than 40 of these from German officials. Thus the League of Nations Council recognised the transfer as final, despite German appeals, and Belgium's existing German border minority was enlarged, creating a trilingual state.

One issue remained in dispute. Despite Belgian efforts, the Commission report of 19 March and decisions of the Four ignored the problem of the Eupen-Malmédy railway, which owing to difficult terrain swung 15 miles (24km) into the German district of Mönschau, zigzagging three times across the frontier and back between the two towns through lightly inhabited territory. The Boundary Commission of the five Powers plus Belgium and Germany was given unusual latitude, and charged to consider economic factors and means of communication. In March 1920, it awarded the railway and intervening area to Belgium. Germany refused to accept this or any subsequent Boundary Commission decision, each giving Belgium less land and even fewer Germans. In November 1922 Belgium and Germany signed a protocol, ratified only in 1931, whereby Belgium gained extraterritorial rights on the railway but none of the intervening area.

Hope of Dutch territorial transfer with compensation from Germany led the Belgian delegation belatedly to investigate what German areas might be transferred. Previously it had only presented the problem to the Great Powers who, in any event, proceeded in the Commission to examine the same districts in Germany's north-western corner. Hymans thought giving this area in exchange for Flemish Zeeland and lower Limburg would provide Holland with more coherent borders. That was true but irrelevant, especially since Belgium was bound by its formal wartime promise not to seek Dutch territory. It remained unaware of the effective Dutch diplomatic drive which had largely dissipated the brief post-armistice hostility to Holland owing to certain non-neutral acts (some born of necessity) and its grant of political asylum to Kaiser Wilhelm II.

Moreover, despite its isolation from Holland and economic ties southward, Flemish Zeeland showed no desire to become Belgian. Its Calvinist majority thought Belgium had too many Catholics, whereas its Catholic minority saw too many Freemasons. In lower Limburg, that tongue of land dipping southward between Germany and Belgium and creating defensive problems for both Low Countries, there was sentiment for attachment to Belgium at the armistice. But the Queen toured and promises were made, causing the movement to subside.

In addition, the Dutch Cabinet would not abandon its Catholic electoral base in Limburg and wanted no German territory, even border districts which were fairly Dutch in character and dialect, lest Germany later seek revenge. An inaccurate press report of Hymans' appearance before the Council of Ten occasioned a formal government statement to the Second Chamber refusing all territorial cession and a query to Hymans, who replied that Belgium had proposed renegotiation of the 1839 Treaties and had asked that Holland participate. He was trying to arrange that the negotiation involved the Great Powers so that Belgium need not face Holland alone. The Dutch were not reassured and multiplied their diplomatic activity in Paris with both the British and the French. Their Foreign Minister, Jonkheer Herman van Karnebeek, who probably shared 'the traditional Dutch disdain for Belgium',[1] privately acknowledged that the territories

> ' ... needs are not rights and create no obligations for third parties.'
> **JONKHEER HERMAN VAN KARNEBEEK**[2]

Hymans sought were exactly those which Belgium needed but remained entirely unmoved.

By the end of February, the Belgian delegation was starting to accept that gaining Dutch areas would be very difficult but did not realise it was impossible. Hymans learned that Balfour had remarked that Holland should not be asked to cede territory. His protest was icily received. The French supported Belgium, but not to the point of jeopardising Dutch loans. Besides, Clemenceau did not favour adding Flemings hostile to France to Belgium's population. House was sympathetic, but Wilson was not. When Hymans saw the Four on 31 March, Wilson said the strategic protection Belgium sought on the Meuse and Scheldt was unnecessary in view of the new League of Nations and German cession of territory to a neutral country would be hard to justify.

The Belgian Commission report of 19 March dealt with the German-Dutch territorial issue because that had to be settled before the Versailles Treaty could be completed. Other aspects of revision of the 1839 Treaties could wait, provided a clause obliged Germany to accept whatever eventuated. The Commission deemed some German areas could be transferred if the inhabitants and the Dutch government agreed. A conditional treaty clause for German consent to future territorial transfer would be necessary and was included. On 16 April Hymans asked the Four to provide such a clause but it chose to do the reverse. It approved the Belgian Commission's report after deleting the clause providing for German territorial cession to Holland. By strong implication, this meant no German compensation to Holland and surely no transfer of Dutch districts to Belgium. In fact, on 4 June the Powers excluded Dutch territorial transfer definitively from future negotiations over the 1839 Treaties.

The question of Luxembourg, which loomed equally large in Belgian eyes, was reserved to the Four. They unanimously wished to end the Grand Duchy's status as a virtual economic satellite of Germany. Probably at first they all sought to dismiss what Clemenceau referred to as the Boche dynasty. Belgium initially hoped to revert to the situation of 1830 wherein Luxembourg was part of Belgium, or at least to gain a dynastic union. However, the rush of events in the Grand Duchy revised Belgian policy, if not that of France.

Why Balfour reserved the complicated but comparatively minor Luxembourg question to the Four instead of sending it to a Commission, claiming it was purely political, is unclear. He was inexact, for the issues were not purely political; the Grand Duchy's flourishing steel industry, railways and mountainous terrain along with the naturally fortified position of its rocky capital city were of economic and strategic importance. Probably he was trying to reduce French influence on decision-making about Luxembourg, in which he failed. One result was that the Luxembourg question was divorced from those of the Rhineland, the Saar, and other German borderlands to which it was related. Another, since Lloyd George's private secretary Philip Kerr (later Lord Lothian) shielded him too well, was that most of Lloyd George's information on Luxembourg came from Clemenceau, the most interested party, who slanted his reports heavily. Throughout, Clemenceau was the only one of the Four who knew of events in the Grand Duchy, though Belgian delegates tried to tell the others.

Some expert analysis of Luxembourg's complicated situation would have been helpful. Foch assigned it to the American occupation zone and remained deaf to frequent Belgian appeals to participate. On 22 November 1918 Marshal Foch himself arrived with an entire French regiment and his staff, declaring Luxembourg City his headquarters. He was rarely there, but the regiment, ostensibly a guard of honour, remained. When in town, Foch carefully went to mass, mitigating local fears of French anticlericalism. The American troops were displaced and most were soon shifted elsewhere. Meanwhile, in December Luxembourg withdrew from the German customs union and its rail convention with the Second Reich; France administered the more important of the two Luxembourgeois railways, which Germany had run.

In early January 1919, a revolution in Luxembourg City led to Marie Adelaide's abdication, exile and replacement by her sister Charlotte. To the disgust of Clemenceau, who wanted a republic, the gallant local French commander ensured Charlotte's accession. She proved to be enormously popular, though it was understood a plebiscite would be held on the future form of government: either the current dynasty, another dynasty or a republic. In February the Chamber unanimously voted to maintain independence. The new Prime Minister, Emile Reuter, sought economic talks with France and Belgium. At Hymans' request, no replies were made.

Neither France nor Belgium had foreseen that Marie Adelaide would go but the dynasty would remain. French policy did not change, and Clemenceau continued to say the 'German' dynasty must go, but Hymans faced reality. Belgium abandoned hopes of annexation or a dynastic tie, only seeking an economic union since Luxembourg must join some neighbour in this respect. Hymans privately hoped for an eventual closer union, but as a distant prospect not affecting his policy in Paris. As both Flemings and Walloons wanted some link, he persisted doggedly through the Conference. His concerns included potential control of trade from Antwerp to the Rhineland, especially if France dominated the latter, bringing a dangerous encirclement of Belgium. His policy did not lack energy but did lack power. He understood the implications of Clemenceau's policy, but owing to his trust in faithful Guarantors, but he could not accept them. His recourse to the British delegation should have succeeded but did not.

In Luxembourg, France imposed a many-faceted press censorship but printed the CPN's annexationist propaganda from the Belgian press and constantly claimed that Belgium intended to annex the Grand Duchy. An intense French propaganda campaign claimed credit for Belgian provisioning of Luxembourg since the armistice, among other lies. Both transportation and communication between Belgium and the Grand Duchy were rendered excruciatingly difficult. Though

France's protected market appealed to some local economic interests, French policy and the attitude of the clergy were probably decisive. They were led to believe that France would protect the dynasty while Belgium would destroy it, though the reverse was true. The longer the French occupation continued, the more opinion in the Grand Duchy shifted toward France. Reuter pursued a complicated course in a tricky situation but consistently sought a three-way economic union. Probably he sought to gain some freedom by balancing between Belgium and France just as Belgium hoped to do between France and Britain.

Hymans knew Clemenceau was annoyed that a small state would oppose him so stubbornly. In fact, the French Premier, who detested Hymans, enjoyed playing cat and mouse with him. He told Mme. Hymans, 'Your husband is a naughty man',[3] and once brutally informed Hymans: 'The best thing you can do for Belgium is die or resign.'[4] He adhered narrowly and steadily to Ribot's 1917 Declaration and said Belgium should have Luxembourg, but added that the present wishes of the Luxembourgeois should be decisive and no defeat should be inflicted on France, two provisos with large implications in the prevailing circumstances. Any original sympathy he may have had for Belgian aims was swamped by pressures from Foch, the General Staff, the Foreign Ministry (where one official talked of resuming the policy of Louis XIV), the steel industry and the sizeable Luxembourgeois colony in Paris along with its adherents in the National Assembly and the Paris press. He consistently delayed to exclude Britain and America, so he could deal with Belgium alone, which is why the debate became prolonged. Luxembourg was a key strategic point on an invasion route into southern Belgium and France, and Clemenceau intended to control it, its steel industry and its railways. When King Albert tried to discuss Luxembourg during his meeting with the Four, Clemenceau's heated diatribe against Belgium, its delegation and Hymans rivalled Lloyd George's eruption a few days earlier.

Pending the dynastic plebiscite, no state recognised Charlotte, and none began economic talks. The French misinformed the Luxembourgeois that the Peace Conference was not dealing with the Grand Duchy whose future was up to its people. Its Cabinet then decided to have an economic plebiscite as well as a dynastic one. Effectively France had arranged to have both under their occupation. When confusion arose over whether the Conference wanted one plebiscite or both delayed, France blamed Belgium for delay of the dynastic plebiscite, though it favoured proceeding and it was Clemenceau who had objected in hope of ending the dynasty. Meanwhile, Belgium and France had embarked on renewed economic negotiations, in which Belgium made concessions but not enough to satisfy France. It was soon clear that economic and military conventions with France were the price of a Belgian solution to the Luxembourg question. If Belgium became a French satellite, it could deal with the Grand Duchy's debts and its worthless German occupation marks, whose redemption was necessary but costly.

In these circumstances, Hymans turned to the British and Americans. Haskins and especially House were sympathetic, but the British were crucial. Well before his clash with Hymans, it was clear that Lloyd George was uninterested in the problem. His elderly Foreign Secretary, Balfour, who murmured, 'A free hand for the little man',[5] and who often dozed through sessions, could be energetic when genuinely interested. On this question he was active, backed by Crowe. From late February on, both sent Lloyd George memos urging support to Belgium about Luxembourg, but without effect or reply. In late March, Crowe proposed that British support to French claims in the Saar basin and Rhineland be made contingent on a Belgian solution to the Luxembourg question. Since Wilson was resisting detachment of the Saar from Germany, this could easily have been done just then, but Lloyd George did not respond and nobody told Headlam-Morley, Britain's member on the Saar Commission. As Wilson gave way on the Saar, the moment passed. The British were poorly coordinated and Lloyd George played a lone hand, whereas the French assigned all west European questions to Tardieu.

Both Hymans and Balfour kept trying while Clemenceau continued to stall. At the end of May, Balfour made two more efforts, and Crowe yet another in June to get a reaction from Lloyd George. Despite Balfour's insistence that the matter was important and pressing, Kerr apparently withheld the memos from Lloyd George who, he said, did not object to Luxembourg joining France. When the Four disbanded, nothing about Luxembourg had been settled, though Belgium successfully blocked a treaty clause assigning the Grand Duchy's railways to France. Despite Balfour's best efforts, Belgium had been defeated by British default, and Belgium had not been put in a position of gratitude to Britain. Lloyd George's hostility to Hymans, his ignorance of the issue and his inclination to ignore his experts contributed to the outcome.

The long-deferred Luxembourgeois plebiscites finally took place on 28 September under French guns and censorship. They yielded the anticipated results for the dynasty and France. By October, Franco-Belgian relations were at an impasse over Luxembourg. Hymans told the French ambassador: *I am ready to negotiate accords ... to bring us together, but on one condition, that they do not endanger our independence. I love France but first of all I am Belgian,*[6] and also, *I know that at Paris I am thought to be clumsy and stumbling. Maybe I don't know how to defend the rights of my country as one might wish, but I plead my cause to the best of my ability... .*[7] The Foreign Office thought that France's treatment of Belgium regarding Luxembourg continued to be deplorable. Intervention on Belgium's behalf was debated but did not take place. Lloyd George apparently placidly assumed Belgium to be a French satellite, thereby leaving it to its own slender resources in its effort to avoid that fate.

As with Luxembourg, the question of colonies was addressed exclusively by the Great Powers since they wanted to keep them all. They made informal allocations in late January but delayed formal action until May so as not to appear greedy. Belgium's colonial goals partook of some of the difficulties of the Dutch question and that of Luxembourg. The territory it wanted belonged to Portugal, an ally. The area it held and perhaps could use to gain its desires was coveted by Britain. And it had revealed its hand to the power whose interests clashed with its own.

The situation was both awkward and complex. Belgium's real concern was the Congo. First, it aimed unsuccessfully at removal of international servitudes imposed upon King Leopold's possession in 1885 and 1890 to gain full sovereignty for development purposes. It also sought to widen the Congo's narrow 25-mile (40-km) Atlantic coast by acquiring at least part of Cabinda and particularly to gain control of the south bank of the River Congo's last seaward leg which belonged to Angola. Both areas were Portuguese, so Belgium could not announce its aims or point out that in theory Portugal could block access upriver to the Congo's capital. Belgium held about a third of German East Africa but wanted none of it, though the inhabitants seemed willing to accept Belgian rule. Its goal was to use this area to gain the desired Portuguese districts via British good offices, with compensation to Portugal from Britain in southern German East Africa and to Britain from the territories Belgium held in northern German East Africa – but that could not be said, either. This complicated manoeuvre required prior formal Belgian possession of former German districts, so at the end of January Hymans sought *free disposition*[8] of Ruanda and Urundi. This phrasing aimed at avoiding a Mandate, since the territory was to be used for trading purposes, but that could hardly be stated to Wilson.

> 'These Belgians have no limits. They are claiming one of the most beautiful parts of East Africa!'
> DAVID LLOYD GEORGE[9]

Belgium's aspirations encountered difficulties not of its own making. In December 1918, the Foreign Office decided that Belgium should not be permitted any part of German East Africa beyond border rectifications. The American delegation agreed, especially its colonial expert, George Louis Beer. Great Powers tended to feel that small states should not have large colonies. Britain in particular wanted all of German East Africa for its planned Cape to Cairo railway, which never materialised. And there was a widespread tendency to confuse King Leopold's undoubtedly malodorous administration with Belgium's reformed regime.

While Hymans supervised negotiations, especially with the Four, those with Britain were conducted by Pierre Orts, a staff member expert in colonial matters. Both men clung in dealing with the Great Powers to seeking 'free disposition' of Ruanda-Urundi, but in March Orts also dealt directly with Lord Milner, the Colonial Secretary, who knew Belgium's real aims. After Orts indicated that Belgium would not evacuate unless it gained satisfaction, Milner agreed to approach Portugal. Nothing more was heard from him.

On 30 April, Hymans learned from the press that German colonies were to be ceded to the five Great Powers. His energetic written protest to Clemenceau brought assurances that this did not prejudge final allocation. But when Clemenceau reported Hymans' letter to the Four, 'Mr. Lloyd George thought it was a most impudent claim. At a time when the British Empire had millions of soldiers fighting for Belgium, a few black troops had been sent into German East Africa.'[10] During further discussion the next day, Wilson remarked that it had been agreed that the Powers would assign Mandates before the League of Nations was established. Lloyd George rejoined, '… to inform M. Hymans of this would be an incitement to him of obstruction'.[11]

There matters rested until the Versailles Treaty was presented to German representatives on 7 May. After the ceremony at the Trianon Palace, Lloyd George gave the other Great Power leaders a list of Mandates, which they hastily approved. The next morning, Hymans learned from the press that Britain had been awarded all of German East Africa. He made an unusual public protest and also expostulated furiously to the Four, saying that Belgium would not recognise this cession. Lloyd George, who knew that Belgium remained in occupation in East Africa, summoned Milner back to Paris. Meanwhile, Hymans asked his own colonial minister to order the Belgian commander in German East Africa to *oppose calmly and with discretion, but also firmly, any attempt to implement this decision on the spot*.[12]

In ensuing negotiations with Orts, Milner pressed to remove Belgium from East Africa, but to no avail. Hymans had learned a few lessons and, for once, Belgium had a card to play, though it did not gain the desired end. Milner admitted that Portugal had rejected the proposed exchange. He saw little point in trying again, especially since there was concern about subjecting more Africans to Portuguese rule. He rejected the compensation Belgium sought for rebuilding the railway and other improvements during its occupation, but allowed certain transport advantages eastward from Belgian territory. As a result, Ruanda-Urundi passed officially to Belgian control on 30 May 1919. Though Beer made further difficulties, the Supreme Council approved the Mandate in August 1919 and the League Council in July 1922.

In Ruanda-Urundi, Belgium received about one-twentieth of German East Africa, but the most densely populated part with three million of the original seven million inhabitants. It continued the German policy of allowing the Tutsi tenth of the Mandate's population to dominate. As the Germans had discovered, the region was not profitable, but it was Belgium's largest territorial acquisition in 1919, largely because it was German and because Belgium was in possession. This unwanted prize dwarfed Belgian territorial gains in Europe. There Belgian acquisitions were less than those of any other continental victor except Portugal (whose wartime role was minimal) and less even than those of neutral Denmark. But Belgium did not wish for any quantity of Germans, who were difficult to assimilate. What it did desire was unobtainable, as was its real goal in Africa. In Europe, more realism at the outset probably would have simplified matters and led to the same territorial result, with less ill will incurred along the way.

6
Economic Issues

Belgium wanted territory, but what it urgently needed was money and especially equipment and raw materials to restart the nation's economy. The situation was dire. Poland and Serbia had also suffered greatly but, being predominantly agricultural, could revive more easily; France's ten richest, most industrial Departments were devastated, but the rest of the country functioned. In Belgium, everything was gone, less from the fighting than from deliberate German action. Since there was no work, the government, which had existed on Allied loans throughout the war, had no choice but to borrow heavily again to keep the citizenry alive amid the ruins. The Commission for the Relief of Belgium provided food, denting the American agricultural surplus, but at a price.

By good fortune, most coal mines survived, though in poor condition and producing at 40 per cent of the pre-war rate. Germany started to flood them, as in France, but Wilson protested during the armistice negotiations, causing it to desist for fear of jeopardising the cease-fire. In addition, the port of Antwerp, unlike Ghent and the coastal ports, was intact though of limited use owing to lack of maintenance and wartime silting in the Scheldt. But that was the extent of the good news. Germany left little else.

In 1917 and 1918, the Second Reich engaged in deliberate destruction of the Belgian economy, dismantling factories altogether and removing whole industries to Germany. During the retreat after the armistice, and in contravention of it, the German army removed everything portable and destroyed what could not be moved. Despite hostile propaganda to the contrary, the desperate condition of Belgium was not in dispute. It was the only country whose damage was systematically surveyed by the United States Army Corps of Engineers.

Metallurgy was completely devastated: most blast furnaces were destroyed, the steel industry entirely halted until midsummer 1919; 85 per cent of industrial production was paralyzed. Most industrial stocks and equipment had disappeared into Germany, down to the last screw, along with livestock, farm machinery, agricultural tools, fertiliser and seed. Rail cars, locomotives and equipment were gone, and the tracks torn up, leaving no transportation network. Moreover, Belgium suffered the most severe price inflation of any West European state. Whitlock, the American envoy, reported: 'Living conditions have been very hard here since our return. The Germans left nothing in the country, and prices have been higher than they would be at the North Pole if two National Political Conventions were suddenly to be held there.' [1]

Belgium's claim to reparation for wartime damage done to civilian property was beyond dispute on the basis of necessity for economic survival and wartime promises by the Great Powers but, as the delegation came to realise, that did not ensure its needs would be met. Reparations presented acute political problems, especially concerning popular expectations in prospective recipient countries, causing the Four to postpone most key decisions. Thus when the Conference ended, Belgium knew neither Germany's total bill nor its own percentage share. In addition, German resources were finite and Great Powers aspired to major shares. Italy had more power and access than Belgium, whose claim was much the largest of the small states. France's needs were unquestionably great, though it could not attack Belgian claims without undercutting its own. Britain could and did so – almost nonstop. American claims were miniscule and it was the only fairly disinterested Great Power. The Belgian delegation wisely turned to Hoover and House, who claimed: 'From the beginning of the Conference, I have made Belgium and her desires my especial care ... and have urged liberal treatment for Belgium at every turn of the negotiations.' [2] Though House had a high opinion of his own diplomatic skills, his claim was largely true and entirely so in regard to reparations. Belgium would have fared poorly without him.

Belgium's two key claims were known as priority and privilege. Priority meant receiving the first German payments to a specified sum in order to restart the economy. Privilege signified relieving Belgium of its pre-armistice debts for the army, the government in exile, and its share of the cost of provisioning the country. These were achieved, though not without considerable struggle, since Britain opposed both. There were additional claims for $537.5 million (£107.5 million) imposed by Germany in forced contributions by the inhabitants, return of stolen paintings and government archives removed to Berlin, and replacement of books, manuscripts and incunabula destroyed in the sack of Louvain. Belgian claims for physical damage proved to be slightly exaggerated, but less so than those of other states. In Belgium, as elsewhere, the public saw no limit to what Germany would pay and it was difficult to estimate costs in rapidly inflating currencies for work over several years.

In addition to physical damage, there was another large financial cost. Germany had forced the population to exchange their Belgian currency for German paper marks at an unfavourable rate. At the War's end, the new Belgian Cabinet said it would redeem them at the same rate. Despite German suspicions, this was done for the sake of the citizenry and of a clean currency, but it was done ineptly. The announcement was made before Belgium had effective control of its borders; thus paper marks poured in from Luxembourg, Germany and especially Holland. Also, the Cabinet assumed pre-war automatic conversion of paper marks to gold marks would resume; it did not, and the gold mark was not used as currency again though it became an essential accounting device for reparations (at four to the dollar and about 20 to the pound) since the value of the paper mark deteriorated rapidly. Thus Belgium held six milliard (each an American billion, a British thousand million) tattered paper marks, for which it sought reimbursement. But other Allies had similar costly supplies of paper marks.

Belgian efforts to attract Wilson's attention to their economic needs roused House's interest; while he substituted for the President during Wilson's absence in America, House tried to settle the question of priority. On 27 February, he told Hymans, saying firmly not to argue, that he and Balfour had decided Belgium should be accorded a reparations priority of $500 million and they would tell Louis-Lucien Klotz, the French Finance Minister, on the morrow. Klotz was willing, but Lloyd George was not. Belgium's economic misery was a factor in his bitter clash with Hymans on 31

March. Lloyd George became particularly angry at mention of Belgium's suffering, complaining that nobody mentioned Britain's suffering.

This situation contributed to King Albert's visit. His talks indicated that Wilson favoured the priority, but Poincaré did not. Lloyd George merely proposed the King's meeting with the Four where Albert began with reparations, reciting stark statistics. Lloyd George was pleasant but evaded decision. House informed his diary: 'I tried to get Lloyd George down to the matter of priority but it was impossible. That was too near accomplishment. I can easily see how the time has been wasted in the Council of Four. They did not come to grips with the King about anything. It was all talk and a promise to look into matters later.' [4]

> 'It is understood that M. Hymans, like other good children, shall be *seen* and not *heard*.'
>
> ARTHUR JAMES BALFOUR[3]

After Albert's visit, Lloyd George continued to argue against Belgian priority, cleverly saying it would be unfair to France. House held firm, threatening public disclosure if need be. The Belgian delegation was neither consulted nor informed of these Great Power disagreements; however, it knew it had received nothing in writing. Then on 23 April, representatives of several smaller states were briefed on the reparations clauses of the draft Treaty. To Belgian dismay, none of their particular concerns were mentioned therein. Belgian protest was so intense that the Three (in the absence of Italy) decided, partly at the instance of House, to hear all the Belgian claims, including the other bone of contention – privilege – on 29 April. After steadfastly refusing to treat Belgium as a special case, the Great Powers finally accepted that it was one.

Privilege presented some of the same difficulties as priority in that neither Britain nor France wanted to wait for reparations. Further, Wilson absolutely opposed inclusion of war costs for any country. By March, all states except Belgium had dropped such claims. Hymans stood on the Declaration of Sainte-Adresse and the Fourteen Points, arguing that Wilson was committed by the latter. Besides, Belgium clearly could not pay all of its four and a half wartime years of expenditure without revenue. Surely, Wilson would make an exception for Belgium.

The audition on 29 April, at which all three plenipotentiaries stood together, launched a critical week for Belgium. The delegation reiterated Belgian reparation claims, addressing priority at length and finally gaining Lloyd George's consent. Privilege, which the Four had been avoiding, was another matter, though Vandervelde stressed that even the Germans admitted they should reimburse Belgium. Lloyd George was adamantly opposed, saying, 'You've had fewer killed than we',[5] Clemenceau was angered by Belgian recriminations, and Wilson was reluctant to make an exception. The delegation gained wartime food costs, but no more. With trembling hands, Hymans said the matter was so grave that it must be laid before the Belgian Parliament and implied that Belgium might not participate in the presentation of the Treaty to the Germans. Lloyd George promptly said, if it did not, all claims on behalf of Belgium would be dropped.

Nonetheless, the Belgian move was superbly timed. Italy had left the Conference; Japan was threatening to do so. If Belgium, the subject of so much wartime oratory and the symbol of the rights of small states, withdrew as well, an already uncertain public opinion in many nations might tip and a general collapse was possible. As a result, privilege was quickly conceded, again with House's helpful assistance, in substance if not in form. It was agreed that Germany would reimburse Allied governments for Belgian pre-armistice debts. Belgium was thus effectively relieved of most of its war debts, though, in the end, American failure to ratify the Versailles Treaty meant Belgium had to re-assume its American debt.

The three plenipotentiaries recommended Belgian acceptance, but the Cabinet wanted inclusion of the paper marks as well. Its rejection led to concession of a seat, which proved important, on the future permanent Reparations Commission to Belgium on all German non-naval questions. Lloyd George continued to complain, saying fewer Belgians than Australians had died, but without effect on Hymans, who was now reinforced by an intense eruption of outrage in the Belgian press all across the political spectrum and the linguistic divide. Typically, *De Standaard* complained: 'It is simply awful how we are treated by our Allies. During four years, … they have wreathed Belgium … in the most beautiful panegyrics and made our heads dizzy with the most glittering promises for the future… . The most serious thing is that our Allies appear to leave Belgium to her misery after she had been owed a debt from the origin of their conflict with the Germans and had been struck even in the very sources of her prosperity.' [6]

Whitlock pointed out that Belgium had lived on hope for four years and now was more depressed than in the war, mainly from fear of economic ruination. The intensity of Belgian opinion rendered Lloyd George's threats to leave Belgium on its own meaningless.

The crisis came to a head on 2 and 3 May, by which time half the Cabinet was in Paris, pressing for concessions. Delacroix and the delegation favoured acceptance, but the Cabinet sought one last try for more concessions, especially on the paper marks and the proposed requirement that Allied post-armistice debts had first claim on sums received as Belgian priority, thereby consuming 40 per cent of it. As a result, Belgium gained return of its state archives and artistic works as well as replacement of literary work. Also, Georges Theunis, a new member of the delegation, wisely insisted that the priority, which was to be stated in French francs, be valued specifically in gold to ensure its continued worth if the franc depreciated.

The Three made their decisions on 3 May, over Lloyd George's protests that 'Belgium was in an extremely favourable position... . In fact the whole priority of Belgium was absolutely indefensible.'[7] Still, it survived though with the Allied post-armistice loans as a first claim. The priority of 2.5 milliard French francs ($500 million, £100 million or 2 milliard gold marks) would be levied on cash payments immediately after occupation costs and those of feeding Germany. After 1 May 1921, it would also apply to deliveries of goods, known as 'kind'. Restitutions of stolen items such as paintings and identifiable livestock were not charged to priority, though replacements were. Priority did not affect the eventual Belgian share of reparations, whatever that might be, but Belgium would 'repay' it by taking a reduced share in later years. Privilege was assured. The delegation urged acceptance, saying no more could be obtained.

Georges Theunis (1872–1966), engineer and financier, handled supply problems in London and Paris during the First World War, served on the Reparations Commission 1919–21, was Minister of Finance 1921–5, and nonparty Prime Minister 1921–5 and 1934–5. A Minister of State from 1925, he served briefly as senator, chaired the World Economic Conference in Geneva 1926–7, and in the Second World War served as a governor of the Belgian National Bank and as special ambassador to the United States. He was known for equanimity, common sense, and a prodigious memory, especially for figures.

But the Cabinet wanted one last try before conceding. Hymans was called to Brussels for a Crown Council. After his two-hour explanation, the Council unanimously accepted the situation on 4 May though no relief had been gained on the first German cash payments and Belgium was left with the six milliard paper marks. So the Belgian delegation attended the 7 May Treaty presentation to a German delegation whose leader stated three times that Germany was willing to redress the wrong done to Belgium. In due course the Belgian Parliament unanimously approved the Treaty.

After 7 May, Belgian delegates had to fight off further inroads on priority and encountered Anglo-French foot dragging. Besides, they had no written guarantee of priority. Privilege had been written into the Treaty (Article 232), and a memo from Hymans to House brought a letter on 16 June from the Four saying that they would recommend to their governments acceptance of German bonds to the amount of Belgium's wartime debt. On priority, Hymans finally appealed to Wilson, who acted. On 24 June the Four signed a formal agreement on Belgian priority.

Belgian opinion was not satisfied. The Brussels weekly magazine *Pourquoi Pas?* (*Why Not?*) caught the national mood: 'Instead of our rights being recognised, they are accorded to us like alms thrown in a fit of temper to a whining child. After we have been told that we represent the Right, Honour, the universal Conscience, Justice and the Ideal; after having been made the cause of the Entente, we are treated as a poor relation, a junior nation, and it is entirely appropriate, when we bring out the Declaration of Sainte-Adresse, if we are told: scrap of paper!' [8]

A British official commented that 'politicians in this country, from Cabinet Ministers to Party hacks, could and did raise cheap cheers ... by promising Belgium payment to the uttermost farthing, and there is no doubt the great mass of Belgians did really believe that we should not sheathe the sword until Belgium had received reparation in full... . The Belgian leaders possibly foresaw that these promises could not be kept ...'.[9] The leaders were not so naïve as the populace, but had not expected such a battle. Both would have been dismayed had they foreseen the struggle ahead. The Belgian war debt was consigned to the London Schedule of Payments of 1 May 1921, though to the ephemeral portion of it, but priority became a bone of Allied contention as greater reparations-hungry states did not wish to wait. The issue contributed to the complex and contentious post-war relations among Britain, France, Italy, Belgium and Germany.

When Belgium finally obtained part of its priority in 1921, it gained deferral of Allied government loans, but most of the initial payment went to repay private British and American banks. By great tenacity, Belgium gained its priority in full by the end of 1925. Thus it did not afford the immediate financial relief for which it was designed. Belgium was restored by its own efforts – and by borrowing. Because Belgium, like other states, assumed that Germany would pay and that priority was certain, it borrowed heavily, contributing to its 1926 financial crisis. Although the economy revived by the late 1920s, Belgium never regained its pre-war prominence in world trade.

German reparations far outstripped other economic issues in importance for Belgium's restoration, but there were additional questions as well. The delegation struggled to gain a share of German merchant shipping and fishing boats. Here the Great Power appetite was large, and though the Belgian claim was firmly based, the state was small and weak.

Ultimately, it gained a share of German river vessels and a small number of merchant ships on reparations account. Nothing could be done about the loss of large pre-war investments in Germany, Russia, Austria and the Ottoman Empire, of which little was recovered. Belgium complained that Allied forces in the Rhineland were being supplied through Rotterdam to the detriment of Antwerp, whose revival was urgent. In March, the United States split its shipments between the two ports; France did the same in May. The British, however, insisted on using Rotterdam almost exclusively.

Britain was equally difficult in other matters. Early in 1919 it made a loan to Belgium (borrowed from the United States) which could be used only for purchase of British manufactured goods, not for the equipment needed to restore production. As Lloyd George kept saying, Belgium was a competitor. Censorship impeded business inquiries, and even the most established Belgian firms had to pay in full before shipment, causing long delays. Over time, Britain continued to withhold machinery and raw materials. As Belgium faced added French pressure for a broad economic agreement, its leaders sought from Britain either imperial preference or a customs union. Though Britain had shown some wartime interest, in May 1919 the Cabinet rejected grant of imperial preference. When Britain saw no Franco-Belgian system would eventuate, it did nothing. Belgian efforts kept encountering Lloyd George's hostility.

The United States was not hostile, but it soon became indifferent. When Wilson visited, he spoke vaguely of the need to restore Belgium but wanted to leave that to private business. He said, 'The proof of the pudding is in the eating',[10] but there proved to be little American pudding to eat, as United States involvement with Belgium declined sharply. Its delegates, especially House, obtained for Belgium its most important economic gains at the Peace Conference in the form of privilege and priority, but both, especially the latter, soon proved to be less than they initially seemed to be.

7
Treaty Revision?

Aside from reparations, Belgium's most important goal at the Peace Conference was revision of the 1839 Treaties. This question was multi-faceted, encompassing territorial questions, compulsory neutrality, the status of Antwerp, the Limburg gap, a new Great Power guarantee and a host of problems involving the Scheldt, the Ghent-Terneuzen Canal and future canals, especially toward the Rhine. Whereas cession of Dutch territory was rendered improbable in April, all other problems remained. Most officials at the Peace Conference assumed treaty revision was simply a routine updating of an obsolete text and were too busy to face the wider implications until later on.

On 16 April, the Four decided treaty revision should not only end limitations on Belgian sovereignty but also 'suppress ... the various risks and inconveniences resulting from the said Treaties'.[1] As Clemenceau and Lloyd George had told King Albert on 4 April that they favoured revision of the Scheldt regime, Hymans had reason for his habitual optimism. He did not know an American official had remarked: 'The new dispositions about to be made by reason of the destruction of the arrangements of 1831–1839 will have to find new safeguards for the independence of Belgium, which by its acts has deserved well of the Society of Nations. It may perhaps be suggested that Belgium has as much to fear from the friendship as from the enmity of its neighbours.'[2]

Hymans aimed to keep the Great Powers, especially the faithful Guarantors, fully involved in treaty revision in hopes that they would exert pressure on Holland, whose viewpoint he did not understand. He genuinely wanted good relations but would have been wise to abandon territorial hopes sooner than he did. He could not see why the Netherlands opposed his proposals to solve Belgium's (and Holland's) security problem, why Dutch opinion became so angry or why the Dutch were reluctant to advantage Antwerp at the expense of Rotterdam. The shrewdest of senior Dutch diplomats opined that seven-eighths of Belgian policy derived from fear of Germany, one-eighth from aspirations to Dutch territory. He thought Hymans was not a strong annexationist but that safeguarding Belgium was a matter of life and death to him.[3] In addition, as treaty revision proceeded by fits and starts, Belgian parliamentary opinion became aroused, despite Hymans' restraining efforts.

At first, however, the situation seemed favourable. On 8 March, the Council of Ten agreed that both Holland and the Great Powers should participate in treaty revision, as Belgium wished. Thus Balfour and Pichon, representing the faithful Guarantors, invited Holland to present its views to the Supreme Council (effectively the Ten and later the Four). After much delay, on 4 April Holland replied: 'The Dutch government considers it understood that the question itself will not be treated by Holland with the Peace Conference in which it does not participate but with the interested powers.'[4] Then and thereafter, the Dutch did all possible to remove negotiations from Paris to The Hague and from the aegis of the Great Powers, whose pressure they feared. The Council of Five, consisting of the five Great Power Foreign Ministers who dealt with lesser matters the Four need not consider, decided they would meet with their Belgian and Dutch counterparts but later on, since they themselves were at present too busy with Versailles Treaty matters and German acceptance of eventual revision of the 1839 Treaties (Article 31) had already been specified.

In the nearly three months which passed before serious negotiations began, the powers most concerned had time to realise that more was involved than simply updating a treaty. The crucial issue was that any real attempt to suppress 'the various risks and inconveniences' to Belgium would create some sort of West European security system. Those most concerned reacted according to their wartime history. Holland and Belgium both sought peace, stability and security, but, after different experiences of the First World War, chose different routes to their goals. Belgium wanted all possible defensive measures and Great Power guarantees, at least from the two faithful Guarantors. The Netherlands consented to join the League of Nations and hoped to house the projected World Court but refused any other international commitment, taking refuge in the neutrality which had protected it to date. France, knowing any guarantee of Belgium constituted effective protection for France, hoped to defend itself in the next war on Belgian soil, sparing its own territory. Britain, on the other hand, was grateful for Dutch neutrality and determined to evade any commitment to defend Belgium (or France) ever again. Since France backed Belgium and Britain supported Holland at every turn, the situation not only embittered Belgian-Dutch relations but aggravated tensions within the Western Entente attempting to deal with the continuing German problem, and thus contributed to the instability of the Peace Settlement.

As treaty revision became drawn out, the idiosyncrasies of individuals contributed to the difficulties. Early on, the American Secretary of State, Robert Lansing, an international lawyer who deemed treaties so sacrosanct that no alteration was tolerable and who had close ties to senior Dutch diplomats, added to Belgian difficulties, as did continuing French pressure toward economic and military accords. Lloyd George's hostility to France and Belgium only deepened over time. As Hymans knew, there were persistent rumours, never substantiated, of heavy Boer pressure on British leaders to abandon any support of Belgium and, later on, some signs that Lloyd George was being difficult about a brief interim guarantee in hopes of gaining French concessions in the Middle East. Moreover, the personalities of the two Foreign Ministers most concerned were incompatible. Hymans was tactless, forthright, dogged and irritatingly precise. Jonkheer Herman van Karnebeek was obstinate, opaque, elusive, secretive, and uncompromising. He viewed Hymans with fear and contempt, but his fear faded when he saw that Belgium did not have much Great Power support.

Jonkheer Herman Adriaan van Karnebeek (1874–1942), a lawyer, was a Dutch official and statesman. He served from 1901 to 1911 in the Department of Colonies, participated in the Second Hague Peace Conference in 1907 and became Burgomaster of The Hague in 1911. As Minister of Foreign Affairs 1918–27, he reorganised the ministry. He was the second President of the League Assembly in 1921, succeeding Hymans, and a member of the Council in 1926. He became a Minister of State in 1927, Queen's Commissioner for the province of South Holland from 1928 to 1942, and a member of the Permanent Court of Arbitration in 1935. He was considered pro-German and extremely difficult to know.

That became obvious when what became known as the Conference of Seven met. In the interim, both parties canvassed for support – the Dutch with greater success. The Belgians expected French aid, knew Lansing was hostile, and thus concentrated on the British, who were consistently sympathetic but excruciatingly vague, dodging any commitment. Hymans concluded that Britain was not very interested and would be of little help. This was an accurate assessment but, as usual, Hymans did not face the implications. He was ever hopeful about the British, and did not recognise that sympathy cost them nothing and gained him nothing. Though he was a lawyer, he did not accept that one formal written commitment was worth more than floods of sympathetic verbiage.

> 'Hymans proceeded by insinuation and allusions rather than by direct arguments.'
>
> JONKHEER HERMANN VAN KARNEBEEK[5]

The Council of Five decided on 9 May that the Conference of Seven would meet on 19 May in Paris. In preparation, the Belgian Cabinet gave Hymans complete freedom to conduct the negotiations as he saw fit but declared that Belgium would accept no territory without full Dutch consent. This latter move, which perhaps should have been made sooner, improved the atmosphere briefly. Nonetheless, Hymans' opening address infuriated van Karnebeek, partly because he sought sovereignty on the Scheldt and the Ghent-Terneuzen Canal and a military servitude for Belgium on the left bank of the Scheldt. Regarding Limburg, he sought unspecified guarantees against the economic and military drawbacks of the existing border, which forced Belgium to defend itself in the middle of the Kingdom. In response, van Karnebeek agreed to ending compulsory neutrality, rejected any territorial cession or military arrangement, and delayed, saying Holland needed time for study since it had no prior information about Belgian grievances. He expected Great Power aid to Belgium would decline when the German phase of the Peace Conference ended and so resisted an international commission, hinting that only in narrow bilateral negotiations in The Hague could Belgium gain anything at all. Hymans, on the other hand, was determined to maintain Great Power pressure on the Netherlands.

After the first session, Hymans provided the Conference with a written statement of Belgian desires, chiefly addressing security questions. Van Karnebeek then called on Hymans, who seemed extremely nervous. This first private meeting, the only one for some years, did not go well, especially as van Karnebeek pressed again for bilateral negotiations and claimed that the Limburg border protected Belgium. Hymans, who knew the Dutch army was as weak as the Belgian army had been in 1910 and that it had withdrawn hastily from Limburg in 1914, wanted a joint military arrangement. After the meeting, van Karnebeek reported: 'I shall see to it that I wriggle ... to a satisfactory way out of the difficult position and arrange it so that the odium, if any, falls to Hymans.'[6]

Additional sessions only demonstrated the total opposition of Dutch and Belgian views. Thus on 4 June the Great Powers met alone. The session turned into a three-hour wrangle between the French and Lansing. When total exhaustion was reached, a sudden resolution gave Belgium the form and Holland the substance. The five Powers would remain involved in treaty revision as to Belgian neutrality and sovereignty (without mention of security) and would establish a Commission which in turn would ask Belgium and Holland to submit joint proposals regarding the waterways.

The Commission itself would study other questions, excluding territorial transfer or imposition of any international servitudes on Holland. Since nobody involved knew what 'international servitudes' meant, the Dutch could reject any unattractive proposal as an 'international servitude'.

Hymans was dismayed, though by now he had abandoned hope of territorial transfer. With reason, he feared treaty revision might become an exercise in nothingness. Crowe thought the phrase about 'international servitudes' might render it impossible. Though he tried to cheer Hymans with hopes of circumventing obstacles in the Commission, privately he wrote: 'We gave away the Belgians when we agreed to Mr. Lansing's demand that nothing should be considered which imposed any servitudes on Holland. The Belgians are not likely now to get anything at all.'[7] The Dutch protested Great Power involvement but were openly jubilant upon return to The Hague, as was the Dutch press.

Hymans decided that Belgium should try to maintain the integral unity of the problem and to keep all aspects of treaty revision and all possible solutions before the Great Power Commission. Accordingly, its acceptance of the Great Power invitation to participate in a new entity consisting of two members from each state and thus known as the Commission of Fourteen included the proviso, citing the Ten's decision of 8 March, that addressing the risks and drawbacks of the 1839 Treaties and ensuring Belgium free economic development and full security not be excluded. Holland also accepted, but with provisos excluding international servitudes and any Commission consideration of measures on which the two states were not in agreement. This last amounted to a Dutch veto. On 25 June, three days before the Versailles Treaty was signed, the Council of Five rejected that. Pichon thought the Commission entitled to try to reconcile differences, but the Great Powers did not constitute themselves as a court and so left little, if any, room for anything Holland opposed.

Owing to Belgian pressure because of Parliamentary agitation, the Commission of Fourteen began work on 29 July with Jules Laroche of the French Foreign Ministry as chairman. The Belgian delegates were Orts and Paul Segers, a senator expert in matters concerning the Scheldt. The Dutch were led by Jonkheer Reneke de Marees van Swinderin, who was both able and experienced. Aside from one Foreign Office representative, most other members were technical experts. There was no dispute about the abrogation of neutrality or permitting Antwerp to become a naval port, though access to it was another matter. Everything else required resolution.

The first six sessions were consumed by an exhaustive exposition of Belgian desires, the seventh by the Dutch rebuttal which, while rather curt, was admirably brief. A Belgian memorandum also enumerated the issues: revised arrangements on all navigable waterways, new security guarantees, access to the Scheldt and Antwerp for Belgian warships in peace and war, joint Belgian-Dutch defence of Limburg and a formal Dutch declaration that invasion of its territory would constitute a *casus belli* (occasion for war). Aside from a few concessions on the waterways, whose negotiation van Karnebeek hoped to remove from Paris, the Dutch delegates had instructions to concede on none of these matters. In addition, the Dutch worried about intense propaganda by the Comité de Politique Nationale in Limburg and unfounded rumours of an impending Belgian raid there. They began to create incidents, including release of an alleged recent letter by Hymans, urging propaganda for Belgian annexation in

Limburg. It was in fact a heavily doctored version of a much earlier memorandum about visa procedures by a minor official, which Hymans could prove he had never seen.

Belgium was determined that these incidents should not end negotiations. Hymans would try to keep the Powers involved in all aspects of treaty revisions and hoped, as Crowe had advised, he could edge around 'international servitudes' if they were never mentioned. However, by this time, Crowe was saying, as the British repeatedly did thereafter, that the League of Nations would provide security for Belgium,

> **England does not want to offend Holland whom she desires to retain in her orbit.**
>
> PAUL HYMANS[8]

though Hymans pointed out that France required an additional guarantee. By midsummer, Britain had become entirely indifferent to Belgian security, despite its historic policy of preventing Great Power domination of the Low Countries, so intense was its fear of embroilment in another Continental war, and it was increasingly unwilling for treaty revision to go beyond the existing treaties. In the ensuing negotiations, France supported some Belgian desires, but Britain none.

After the Dutch presented their case and abruptly went home, the Great Powers decreed that technical arrangements for the navigable waterways should be decided by Belgian-Dutch negotiation, as Holland wished. Belgium yielded without protest, aware that Holland would obstruct any other procedure indefinitely. Other matters, including the various aspects of Belgian security, would be handled by the full Commission. In fact, the full Fourteen met rarely thereafter. Anglo-French wrangles occurred in meetings of the five Great Powers or in their military and naval subcommittee.

In contrast, the Belgian-Dutch fluvial discussions seemed

to go well at first. These concerned such matters as pilot-age, lighting, buoys, construction, sanitary arrangements, telegraphy and especially dredging to maintain or deepen the channel. Under the existing treaty, Holland was obliged to maintain the channel, but did not, and only permitted Belgium to do so under crippling restrictions, despite an obvious need to deepen the channel for larger vessels. Holland also limited use of Belgian pilots. Because the Dutch feared Great Power pressure, Belgium gained some improvements which never came into effect.

The Dutch were adamantly opposed, however, to any Belgian naval access to the Scheldt or joint defence of Limburg and very reluctant about a *casus belli* clause. As Britain increasingly assumed that nothing should be done against Dutch wishes, treaty revision dwindled. British offi-cials said small states should not have large navies and Zee-brugge would suffice for a Belgian navy of two or three small ships; they knew the Limburg problem was real but refused to face it. Only the War Office looked realistically at West European security problems, but it was not involved in these negotiations. On the whole, since Britain did not want to defend Belgium again, it had no desire to render it defensible. Meanwhile, Laroche and his British counterpart dealt separately with the Dutch and Belgians. France devised various ingenious combinations, but each amounted to a form of West European security pact, which Britain wished to avoid.

Finally, Laroche gained an agreed statement of the five Great Powers that merely ending obligatory neutrality and the old guarantee would not suffice as it would provide Belgium with no security and would increase the instability of the peace. Moreover, '... the Allied and Associated Powers

... consider that they could not morally put their signature at the foot of a treaty of revision abolishing the neutrality of this country unless Belgium were to receive other guarantees which would in some way replace the old or rather would guard against the disadvantages which would result for her from the suppression pure and simple of perpetual neutrality'.[9] When Laroche formally read this statement to the Fourteen on 16 September 1919, the Belgians, who were unaware of the lengthy semantic struggle behind it, took it as a promise of new guarantees, which it was not.

At British instigation, the Dutch, who worried that their refusal to surrender the Kaiser would cause Great Power pressure, consented to join the League of Nations, accept a *casus belli* clause and declare that they would defend Limburg. As it became clear, however, that the Kaiser would not be introduced into the negotiations though Lloyd George was seeking his trial, and that Belgium had little Great Power support, they reneged on the latter two commitments. The British blamed Hymans for the situation, mainly because they did not want to defend Belgium and wanted the question to go away. Hymans was increasingly dogged and in some respects more irritating as one promise after another evaporated, but the problem was neither of his making nor within his capacity to solve. Nobody at the Belgian Foreign Ministry realised that Britain was trying to revert, as much as the Versailles Treaty would permit, to its 19th-century position at the centre of the balance of power. Lloyd George would make no commitment to either side, but thought Germany was the weaker power and needed bolstering at French expense, a view impacting Belgium as well. The United States was withdrawing from Europe. Neither Anglo-Saxon power would pressure Holland as Laroche desired. Thus Hymans was blamed for pursuing the security the Great Powers said was essential to the peace but did not wish to provide.

As it was soon clear nothing would be done about the Limburg gap or Belgian naval access to the Scheldt, negotiations in the autumn focused on Belgian security in general. To the weary delegates, it seemed easiest to refer the problem to the League Council. Hymans thought it unlikely that a body dominated by the same five Powers as were represented on the Fourteen would be more likely to provide a substantial guarantee and perhaps less so if Germany joined the League; besides, Belgium would be defenceless in the meantime. Thus on 16 October Belgium declared its public and Parliamentary opinion would not accept the proposed treaty unless the two faithful Guarantors continued the 1839 guarantee of Belgium's independence and territorial integrity (but *not* neutrality) until the League provided new guarantees. This set off a long, confused debate about an interim guarantee. It was complicated by simultaneous negotiations about adding Belgium to the Anglo-American guarantee of France agreed at the Paris Peace Conference, and others about adding Britain to Franco-Belgian military talks. Hymans kept the three negotiations, all designed to the same end, entirely separate, but British officials occasionally became confused.

France was willing to provide an interim guarantee, as was the Foreign Office at first. Belgium accepted a draft treaty providing one until the League created another but also wanted the Dutch *casus belli* clause. The Foreign Office and Lord Curzon, who had replaced Balfour as Foreign Secretary in October, decided the interim guarantee should be limited to five years, claiming British public and Parliamentary opinion would reject more. This was the first of many such references, though no hostility to a guarantee was ever discernable. The

Cabinet, however, wanted to know whether the United States might participate and whether it would ratify the guarantee of France. As both looked unlikely, British interest waned though, as all concerned knew, there would be no threat to Belgium during the next five years while British forces were in the Rhineland at Cologne.

On 19 November, the very day of the first rejection of the Versailles Treaty by the American Senate, France pointed out that Belgium would reject a treaty without a guarantee and thus the old treaty with its guarantee would remain in force. This sobered the British, especially as one official remarked that it was British policy 'to contract no new obligation towards Belgium which will mean the protection of the French frontier coterminous with Belgium'.[10] Curzon preferred the 1839 Treaty and, in any event, wanted Belgian neutrality as the price of a guarantee. He seemed to think there must be a price, may have hoped to detach Belgium from France though British policy otherwise tended to impel Belgium toward the French or may have preferred what Belgium was sure to reject as a route to escaping continental commitment altogether. The matter was discussed on 2 December in a Cabinet conference whose minutes are cryptic. It was unclear what Britain meant by neutrality, or what benefit neutrality would give Britain. The discussion started with a five-year guarantee without neutrality and somehow ended with a guarantee of neutrality until the League of Nations was created (i.e. within a few months), which Belgium was sure to reject.

By December 1919 the economic and fluvial arrangements were set, Holland had agreed to a diluted *casus belli* clause and seemed prepared to conclude, and the only real problem was British insistence on neutrality. As news came that Curzon was adamant about this and that Lloyd George, Balfour and

Andrew Bonar Law, the Conservative leader, all opposed a guarantee, Laroche's several efforts to concoct a treaty satisfying both Britain and Belgium failed. On the advice of Hymans, who said the five-year guarantee was worthless, on 5 January 1920, five days before the Versailles Treaty came into force, the Belgian Cabinet unanimously agreed to withdraw the request for a guarantee, abandoning hope that the 16 September Great Power declaration would be fulfilled.

Accordingly, Laroche prepared a new draft which abrogated the neutrality clause, registered the new economic and fluvial arrangements and contained a Dutch *casus belli* declaration. Treaty revision had come to no more than this. There were signs, however, that the Dutch might make difficulties over both the *casus belli* clause and the Wielingen Channel, the southernmost of the Scheldt's three mouths and the only one deep enough for large ships. It turned south, sweeping the Belgian coast to Blankenberge, and much of it was within Belgium's three miles (4.8km) of territorial waters. The question of the Wielingen Channel had never been resolved; in 1839 and thereafter, it had been agreed that sovereignty would not be specified, though the Dutch had stated four times during the First World War that it was not theirs. In the current negotiations, it had been agreed to leave the matter in abeyance, as in the past.

When the Fourteen met on 23 March 1920 to resolve matters, however, van Swinderin departed from the prearranged text and made the first formal Dutch claim to exclusive and full sovereignty on the Wielingen Channel in Belgian history. Nobody took the claim seriously, and van Swinderin admitted privately that Holland was on 'very brittle ice' in the matter.[11] After it reiterated its claim in a formal note on 3 May, Belgium broke off negotiations until the Wielingen dispute was resolved. If it were not, the possibility arose of no wartime access to Zeebrugge, Belgium's only deep-water coastal port. One Belgian official later wrote, '… the Belgian government in refusing to sign acted primarily under the impulse of spite and anger after the repeated checks received in the revision negotiations'.[12] Possibly this was so, and possibly the Wielingen dispute could have been resolved, but another issue might well have arisen in its place. Hymans himself said: *The Belgian government cannot accept a claim which would entail a disruption of the national territory and a diminution of the country's national security.*[13] The British, French and Belgians all thought the Dutch had raised the Wielingen question to avoid concluding a treaty, and, for Belgium, losing any hope of wartime succor was too high a price to pay for slightly improved fluvial arrangements. In fact, the Dutch were astonished at the Belgian action. They too had lost perspective, particularly since 90 per cent of Belgian opinion supported Hymans, especially the Flemings whose coast was at issue. At Belgian insistence, an Anglo-French demarche at The Hague was arranged, but van Swinderin managed to delay it to the point that it never took place. The Commission of Fourteen ended by noting the two viewpoints and the impossibility of bridging the gap.

The issue lingered through the summer, but various proposals achieved nothing. Hymans resigned in August over unrelated matters. Delacroix, who replaced him at the Foreign Ministry, made a new effort. The Dutch genuinely tried to be conciliatory, but their concessions were insufficient in Belgian eyes. Britain now took the view that the matter was entirely up to the Belgians and Dutch and refused any Great Power action. By October it was clear that Delacroix had failed, and he resigned soon thereafter. In 1921 the new Cabinet made a brief effort which came to nothing.

As a result, the 1839 arrangements between Holland and Belgium remained in effect. Belgian neutrality was not abrogated in the Versailles Treaty or any other document but died a *de facto* death as Belgium joined the League of Nations, remained engaged in the Rhineland occupation and sought military accords with Britain and France. With the passage of time, it was assumed that the old guarantees had died as well. Thus years of Belgian effort gained nothing. In this as in other matters, Hymans made mistakes, but they were not crucial. Britain's attitude toward France and its misreading of the power balance had decided the matter. On 16 September the Powers had said that failure to provide new security to Belgium would increase the instability of the peace; this it did, as the Western Entente struggled to find any agreement at all.

As the promised revision of the 1839 Treaties had gained Belgium nothing, so with other issues. In most respects, Belgian expectations had been disappointed. Belgium emerged from the Peace Conference without the Dutch districts to which it had naively aspired. The territorial truncations of 1839 remained, as did the security problems. The old Great Power guarantee seemed to be gone, but nothing had replaced it. There was no defensive arrangement for the Limburg gap, and equally the question of Luxembourg was still unresolved. Belgium had gained Ruanda and Urundi, which it did not want, but not the African territory it did want. Two Walloon Cantons and Moresnet were small solace after four agonising years. True, there would be reparations, but how much and when? In the meantime, the Allies were not helping appreciably with the promised restoration of a devastated country. As Pierre Orts said: 'We awoke to reality in order to confirm the loss of all our illusions.'[14]

Paul Hymans the first President of the League of Nations

III

The Legacy

8

The Search for Security

At the Paris Peace Conference, few of the major Belgian claims were resolved with much permanence. The optimistic hope of Dutch territory had been definitively excluded, but most other issues were either unsettled or tended to become newly unsettled with dismaying frequency. When the Big Four left at the end of June 1919 as the German phase of the Conference ended, Eupen-Malmédy and the Belgian aspect of reparations (to a degree) seemed settled, but the marks question was unresolved, as were Luxembourg and the issue of security guarantees. The latter two soon merged and the others kept arising. Under the circumstances, Belgian diplomacy in the 1920s and sometimes later was based to a large extent on the lacunae and instability of the Peace Settlement.

Belgium's post-Treaty goals included formal recognition of the end of obligatory neutrality and the revision of the 1839 Treaties, then supposedly in progress. It was anxious to settle reparations to know its share and to gain funds for economic reconstruction. Above all, it sought new security guarantees to replace the old. As Hymans later wrote: *The concern which entirely dominated Belgian foreign policy at*

Europe 1923

FINLAND

Petrograd (St Petersburg)

Tallinn
ESTONIA

Riga
LATVIA

LITHUANIA

Königsberg
EAST
PRUSSIA

Vilnius

Warsaw

Brest-Litovsk

POLAND

Kiev

UNION OF SOVIET
SOCIALIST REPUBLICS

Moscow

VAKIA

Budapest

GARY

ROMANIA

Odessa

Belgrade

Bucharest

SLAVIA

BULGARIA

Sofia

Black Sea

ANIA

Istanbul

GREECE

Athens

TURKEY

IRAQ

SYRIA

CYPRUS

*the end of the War and in the post-war era was that of secu-
rity, necessarily linked to that of independence.*[1] When the
Delacroix Cabinet was reconstituted in December 1919, the
ministerial declaration promised that Belgium would continue to depend upon the bloc of Western Powers, especially
France and Britain. Hymans elaborated to the Chamber that
the *idea ... to conclude with the two great Western Powers,
France and England, military arrangements which will assure
our defence corresponds to the common interests of the three
countries. Belgium protects the northern frontier of France
and the North Sea coast.*[2] His belief that Belgium's safety
was of common concern to all three countries was sensible
but futile in the prevailing circumstances. All Belgian leaders,
however, still expected early guarantees.

The First World War had been fought in part to preserve the
pre-war balance of power which, among other functions, protected Belgium. Instead, the war destroyed that balance, and
the Peace Conference provided nothing to replace it, partly
because Wilson was hostile to any mention of the balance of
power, which he considered evil. In the new Europe where the
Habsburg Empire had collapsed, Germany was temporarily
stricken and Russia a distant pariah, what remained was an
Anglo-French impasse, which gave Belgium prominence but
not the security it craved. Its policy of Anglo-French-Belgian
entente was a direct result of the war as well as a habitual reli-
ance on the faithful Guarantor Powers. Like France, Belgium
needed security and reparations. Like Britain, it sought a
renewal of world trade and a European balance of power.
But it found itself in a delicate position between a Britain and
a France whose policies clashed in most respects.

One might ask why Belgium was so preoccupied with
security when it was clear, even before the negotiations for

revision of the 1839 Treaties, that there was no immediate danger. Such concern was predictable in an exposed small state with powerful neighbours, particularly in view of recent history. Habit of mind entered into it, as did craving for full economic freedom to restore Belgium's trading position. And a guarantee would probably be easier to obtain before danger approached. The psychological

> 'Briefly in the mind of the French Government the destiny of France and that of Belgium were inseparable.'
>
> ANDRÉ TARDIEU[3]

effect of standing alone against Germany was unnerving, even if the immediate danger was slight: Belgium *felt* insecure. None of its leaders, and no statesmen elsewhere, seem to have contemplated the improbability of real territorial security in that crowded corner.

Belgian leaders, including Hymans, were naïve in assuming that new guarantees to replace the old could be had for the asking, but the dismal 1839 Treaty negotiations did not dampen their optimism appreciably. In fact, a guarantee could probably have been obtained easily at the Peace Conference had Hymans been better and sooner informed. It would have availed little, however, since it would have been part of the American guarantee of France which was never approved, causing the concomitant British guarantee to lapse.

The Anglo-American guarantee of France was first proposed by Lloyd George on 14 March 1919 in a successful effort to deter French plans to detach the Rhineland from Germany. The first French written reply on 17 March contained a postscript: 'It goes without saying that by act of aggression against France, the French government understands also any aggression against Belgium.' [4] The United States at the time assumed the same, but nobody told Hymans then or later.

He first heard rumours at the beginning of May. Tardieu confirmed these, adding that he expected Clemenceau would tell Hymans about the guarantee within two or three days. Clemenceau did not do so, and the Great Power negotiations did not include any discussion of Belgium. Although House was out of favour with Wilson by this time, he probably could have arranged Belgian inclusion if anybody had thought of it or Hymans had asked promptly. At a closed plenary session on 6 May, Tardieu informed the Conference of the Anglo-American guarantee of France. A senior French diplomat urged Hymans to speak up about including Belgium, but he wisely did not, instead inquiring at the French Foreign Ministry (the Quai d'Orsay). Tardieu explained that France had gained the guarantee at the last minute and Clemenceau wanted a little time to lapse before extending it.

The very next day, however, Clemenceau sent word via Tardieu that he wanted to discuss the matter within a few days and was willing to travel to Brussels to settle with King Albert. Hymans concluded that France in fact was seeking a Franco-Belgian military accord and was less concerned with an Anglo-American guarantee of Belgium. This proved to be the consensus among Belgian leaders, who by now had learned a few lessons. Delacroix felt the price would be too high, especially regarding reparations, over which Belgium had fought intense battles just the week before. Thus Belgium did not take up Clemenceau's offer.

On 28 June both the Versailles Treaty and the Anglo-American guarantee of France were signed, the latter after Lloyd George had quietly arranged that the British treaty would take effect only if the American one did as well. In late June, Clemenceau gave Hymans the texts of the guarantee treaties and proposed extension to Belgium with France as a third Guarantor. Hymans remained wary, and King and Cabinet decided not to act. But as problems arose over revision of the 1839 Treaties and the Versailles Treaty was safely signed, ensuring that no concessions could be demanded as to its clauses, concern mounted in Brussels.

During a French ceremonial visit to Liège in late July, Hymans specifically sought a trilateral guarantee to replace that of 1839. In late August in Paris, he tried again, but by then France clearly preferred a Franco-Belgian accord. Hymans turned to Britain, inquiring about extending the Anglo-American guarantee of France to Belgium. The Belgian envoy sent an optimistic report, so Hymans raised the question with Poincaré in mid-September, hinting that Luxembourg must be settled first. On 20 September Hymans formally requested British and French extensions of the guarantee to Belgium. Since King Albert was touring the United States (where enthusiastic Yankee crowds often addressed him as 'Hey, King!'), he raised the matter with Lansing, who said that if the Senate approved the French treaty, there would be no problem in extending it to Belgium. Soon thereafter, Britain ratified its guarantee of France. Belgian leaders were briefly optimistic.

In mid-October, however, Curzon began saying British opinion would not accept a guarantee of Belgium. He realised the American guarantee might fail and he did not want any unilateral continental commitment. The British press supported Belgium, but the government did not. In November, Lansing said the time was not opportune to discuss a Belgian guarantee. Later that month, the United States Senate rejected the Versailles Treaty for the first of two times. It never voted on the French guarantee treaty. As American approval of the Versailles Treaty became unlikely, the idea of a tripartite guarantee of Belgium quietly died, along with hope of an interim guarantee in connection with revision of the 1839 Treaties. That left only the least attractive route to security, the Franco-Belgian military accord, which itself potentially threatened Belgian independence. In fact, Hymans wanted a French guarantee but only in conjunction with a counterbalancing British one to placate the Flemings and to protect Belgium from French domination. Therein lay the difficulty.

France had decided early in the First World War that Belgium was to become its satellite and its battleground in the next war. This had become obvious as France pursued its aim in a variety of ways. One reason Hymans tried so desperately to settle matters during the Peace Conference was that he greatly feared Belgium would be left alone soon to cope with France unilaterally, as happened. He knew that a small country with few, if any, bargaining counters was at a great disadvantage.

On 25 August 1919, Clemenceau abruptly summoned Hymans to Paris. By then, in ongoing economic negotiations, Belgium had accepted a metallurgical cartel, France's main desire, and a few other French demands, but, despite its lack of much to offer, it still resisted a preferential tariff forcing free-trading Belgium to increase duties on goods from other countries, especially Britain, one of the issues along with the surtax and rail questions on which the talks ultimately failed in October. For the moment, however, the prospects of economic agreement looked good. Clemenceau said that since an economic accord was close, he would advise Luxembourg to turn to Belgium for an economic union. Hymans' delight quickly turned to consternation when Clemenceau added that France would keep the Guillaume-Luxembourg railway and expected a Franco-Belgian military convention.

It is striking that Clemenceau saw Hymans personally, summoning him in vacation season, rather than having Pichon tell the Belgian envoy. He clearly wished to relish Hymans' dismay. After the leading Anglo-Americans left Paris, neither he nor his senior staff bothered to be polite or even civil about Luxembourg, verging at times on real brutality. Belgium consistently rejected French terms, as Foreign Ministry, Cabinet, and King unanimously did in August. Whenever tension became acute, Pichon would offer soothing phrases and promises which were never kept. From this point on, the question of Luxembourg and that of a military accord were inextricably entangled. And after August 1919, talks focused primarily on the Grand Duchy's railways.

Europe's pre-war experience, chiefly German rail construction in the Ottoman Empire, had demonstrated that control of a nation's railways could lead to political domination. Certainly, France's presence in Luxembourg could impede any eventual political union, of which Hymans had lingering hopes. And France could potentially restrict Belgian rail traffic to the south and east. Economic union, which Hymans was pursuing primarily to remove Luxembourg from the French orbit, was not economically desirable without the profitable railways, especially since in most respects the Grand Duchy's industry and agriculture competed with their Belgian counterparts.

There were two Luxembourgeois rail companies; of these, the Société Prince-Henri (the less important), to whose control France aspired, was Brussels-based and under Belgian administration. The other, the Société Guillaume-Luxembourg, headquartered in Paris with more French capital than Belgian, was the object of contention. Aside from pressuring Belgium toward a military accord, France's interest

was strategic and economic. The Guillaume-Luxembourg
network consisted of short but vital segments of major east-
west and north-south international routes. It served Western
Europe's main iron and steel complexes in the Ruhr, southern
Belgium, southern Luxembourg, Lorraine and Longwy, and
provided the best route for delivery of reparations coal from
the Ruhr to Lorraine. As a senior French official frankly said:
'Luxembourg has a crucial importance for us: it is one of the
global meeting places of coal and iron, that is to say, of domination of the world.' He added that the price of French dis-
interest was for Belgium to enter 'our financial, military, and
customs orbit'.[5] The Guillaume-Luxembourg railway was an
invasion route into France but Belgium was a more dangerous invasion route. Foch and other French officials openly
distrusted Belgian ability and willingness to defend itself and
the Grand Duchy.

By the time of the Luxembourg plebiscites in September,
all Franco-Belgian negotiations were near deadlock. The
outcome only strengthened France's hand. Clemenceau flatly
refused to talk about the railway, saying the French decision was final. The Belgians were astonished. After they had
blocked award of the railway to France at the Peace Conference, it had not been mentioned during the economic
negotiations and they had naively assumed France had abandoned its claim, though the railway had been under French
military administration since the armistice. Hymans sought
compromise, despite a strong legal claim on the Guillaume-
Luxembourg east-west line. He and Reuter agreed that the
railways and the custom union should go together, but he
offered France a joint administration and informal wartime
military rights, to no avail. France claimed the Guillaume-
Luxembourg network under clauses of the Versailles Treaty

about Alsace-Lorraine, which clearly did not apply, and was frank that it would control Luxembourg's steel and railways and force Belgium and Luxembourg together into sweeping economic and military pacts committing Belgium to the defence of France. It threatened, especially during the 1839 Treaty negotiations, to block any Allied security guarantee of Belgium unless its terms were met. As relations became very bitter in late September, Hymans erupted to a French official: *In the final analysis you want to take Luxembourg. Take it, since you are the stronger. But you will take it against us. Belgium will remember.*[6]

As Belgian independence was at stake, Hymans turned to Britain. The Foreign Office agreed that the French legal argument regarding the Versailles Treaty was absurd. A protest to Paris was drafted but quashed because of its potential effect on delicate negotiations then in progress over Syria. Thus Hymans gained much sympathy, but no help. By the end of 1919, Franco-Belgian relations were extremely poor. Hymans kept Britain fully informed, but it took no advantage of the situation. It was not much interested in Luxembourg or in Belgium, which it placidly assumed to be a French satellite while Hymans struggled to escape that fate. His only asset was French fear of alienating a necessary ally on the invasion route into France. He insisted that satisfactory arrangements for Luxembourg must be completed prior to any military accord (whereas France said the reverse) and fought doggedly on, believing that something helpful would turn up because it must.

In January 1920, Clemenceau was replaced by Alexandre Millerand, who served as his own Foreign Minister, and a personnel shift occurred at the Quai d'Orsay. These changes thawed relations somewhat, but when Hymans said at a high level Franco-Belgian conference that a military accord should be *the crowning act of arrangements on the essential questions which France and Belgium have discussed for several months*,[7] a new chill set in. By April of 1920, however, France became more accommodating because it found itself in need of diplomatic support. The something Hymans had been hoping for had arrived, thanks to events in Germany.

On 13 March in Berlin, irregular forces displaced the legal government and established a new regime under Wolfgang Kapp. This *Putsch* lasted four days before the Weimar Cabinet regained control. By prior agreement, it still had forces in the Rhenish demilitarised zone but asked to send more to deal with an alleged 'Red Revolution' in the Ruhr basin. As there was no Allied agreement, it received no reply and so sent troops on 20 March and 2 April without authorisation. On 1 April, Millerand promised Britain that France would not act alone. On 4 April, however, it did just that and by 6 April had occupied Frankfurt and four neighbouring towns. Its allies had been notified but had not consented.

On 4 April Millerand sought Belgian support. Hymans underestimated British rage, not expecting British endorsement or participation, but vainly hoping for no public disavowal of France. On 7 April France suddenly accepted his latest formula for the Guillaume-Luxembourg railway and military talks. Thereupon Hymans told the Cabinet that backing British opposition, as requested on 8 April, would obtain nothing, but supporting France would gain them Luxembourg. Besides, as much Allied unity as possible was needed *vis-à-vis* Germany; joining France would prevent its isolation and perhaps restrain it. Thus he recommended Belgium send troops to Frankfurt provided the occupation ended when German troops left the Ruhr and with clear indication that pending questions, especially Luxembourg, would be settled satisfactorily. As the Cabinet agreed unanimously, a Belgian battalion entered Frankfurt on 14 April, leaving on 17 May as Germany evacuated its extra troops from the demilitarised zone.

While these events were in progress, Hymans had, especially in March 1920 before Belgium had to choose between Britain and France, done all possible to persuade London to participate in some form of military talks, saying: *If in the future I were to tell the Chamber that we proposed a military entente to France and England, that France accepted and England refused, the moral effect would be deplorable. Belgium has always considered England as its real friend. Belgian statesmen are convinced that Belgian security should rest on the double foundation of French and British amity. It should not be a matter of indifference to England if Belgium relies exclusively on France.*[8]

He rashly tried again at a Supreme Council, one of the periodic meetings of the European Great Powers, held at San Remo in late April, only to discover Curzon was furious to find Belgium where he had always assumed and encouraged it to be, at the side of France. Further efforts also failed, and relations with France were bumpy. Talks about the Guillaume-Luxembourg railway began on 23 April, as Luxembourg learned from the press. Belgian distrust of Reuter was such that Hymans had no hesitation in doing unto others what had been done to him at the Peace Conference, though as a face-saving measure he promised that the Grand Duchy, while excluded from the Franco-Belgian talks, could participate in the final arrangement.

A Franco-Belgian commission of experts quickly settled on a Belgian proposal dating from September 1919 and informally agreed on 9 May to divide the network, giving France control of lines most important to it south and east of Luxembourg City and shifting the rest to Belgian administration. Luxembourg disliked division of the railway but was helpless to prevent it. On 10 May Millerand said France would not join a customs union and it should turn to Belgium. There were difficulties over details of the 9 May informal agreement, especially France's demand for a formal written promise it could use all the railways in wartime. Hymans pointed out that Belgium could not give formal permission to violate Luxembourg's neutrality but could do nothing more than protest if a violation occurred. On 26 May Belgium and France reached a formal agreement on the railway in the presence of Grand Ducal representatives, France having yielded on financial issues and the written promise.

Negotiations for a Belgian-Luxembourgeois customs union began in June 1920, reaching fruition with the railway question reserved in an agreement on 17 May 1921 after Hymans left office. Belgium had supported France at a London Supreme Council in late April and early May 1921 and in return France had secretly renounced its rights on the Guillaume-Luxembourg network subject to wartime use. Negotiations also began on 10 June 1920 between Foch and General Henri Maglinse, the Belgian Chief of Staff, toward a military accord. Simultaneously, Hymans tried for British consent to a plan without commitment which could be used when and if Britain decided to act in a war. The War Office, which was conducting unauthorised staff talks with France and Belgium, strongly favoured this, but on 30 June the British Cabinet decided that 'the proposed military conversations would be premature at the present time'.[9]

Still, Belgium would not sign the military accord without a

final attempt to gain British involvement. At a brief conference in Brussels at the start of July 1920 prior to the Spa Supreme Council, Lloyd George announced his refusal to the press and confirmed it on 12 July at Spa to Delacroix, arguing that there was no danger for 20 years and saying: 'Believe me, it is premature.'[10] Thereupon Delacroix, Hymans and Henri Jaspar took the decision on 16 July to accept the accord, which was signed by the generals on 29 July, though the definitive version was only completed on 7 September.[11]

The French tended to view the accord as an alliance, the Belgians as a narrow technical arrangement without obligatory force. The truth lay somewhere between the two. The text of the accord remained secret and was not ratified by the Belgian parliament, as was required for treaties. Only the identical cover letters exchanged between the two parties were published and registered at the League of Nations, as the Covenant embodied in the Versailles Treaty required for treaties and international engagements. Belgium, where the accord was unpopular with Flemings and Socialists, stressed that the cover letters specified that the sovereignty of each party remained intact as to both military expenditure and deciding whether the accord applied in a given instance.

Henri Jaspar (1870–1939), a lawyer and Catholic statesman, became Minister of Economic Affairs in November 1918 and Minister of the Interior from June to November 1920. He was Foreign Minister from late 1920 to 1924 and again from June to November 1934. Prime Minister from 1926 to 1931, he became Minister of Finances from 1932 to 1934, Minister of Colonies in 1927–8 and again in 1928–31 and Minister of State in 1931. He presided over both Hague Conferences in 1930 and 1931. A small man closely resembling Lloyd George, he was sensitive to personal slights, not those to Belgium. He and Hymans were not close, but their policies were nearly identical. Aside from Vandervelde's foreign ministry in 1925–7, they dominated inter-war Belgian foreign policy. (See *Henri Jaspar, Portrait d'un homme d'état* by Georges Sion.)

The secret accord applied to the case of unprovoked German aggression. That in theory might be against Poland, though most of the text dealt with Franco-Belgian actions in the occupied Rhineland in response to a German threat of aggression or general mobilisation. These aspects were clearly technical, but in anticipation of the Rhineland occupation's end there would be staff talks about a common frontier defence, including that of Luxembourg (without its consent). In addition, the French navy was entitled to defend the Belgian coast.[12] It was unclear whether Belgium need act if France alone were invaded or whether French troops could enter Belgium if Germany created acute diplomatic tension. The accord did not lead to regular staff talks or military coordination.

According to Delacroix, Hymans was the chief partisan of the accord, despite the absence of Britain (which was informed and invited to join) and of a Franco-Belgian commercial agreement. He felt Belgium could not stand entirely alone. One of his few critics in Belgian diplomatic circles charged: 'After the defeats and disillusionments of Versailles, M Hymans wanted a success.' [13] Perhaps, but Luxembourg was probably more important. In the course of negotiation about it, he told the French ... *there is always a danger for a small country in being encircled by a larger one. Belgium has need of air and her freedom of movement. She does not want to be absorbed in any manner, dominated, or morally and economically penetrated.*[14] He always insisted the accord was not an alliance, and his lawyerly mind saw the cover letter as excluding legal obligation, though whether it excluded moral obligation was more questionable.

Hymans was also too trusting, as ever, of a faithful Guarantor Power. The absolute condition of the military accord was Luxembourg, but France did not honour its promises. It retained the entirety of the Guillaume-Luxembourg network and kept its troops in the Grand Duchy. During the occupation of the Ruhr, when France acutely needed Belgian support, insistence from Brussels extracted the French troops from Luxembourg in December 1923, but France controlled the railway in full until the German invasion of 1940. Hymans resigned over an unrelated matter shortly after the decision at Spa but returned to office in 1924 and negotiated a new rail convention, which the Luxembourgeois Chamber rejected. No matter: France still held the railway.

The accord with France remained Belgium's sole defensive agreement for several years. In January 1922, when a Franco-British treaty was under consideration, Jaspar as Foreign Minister negotiated a parallel treaty with Britain which achieved an agreed text and consent of both Cabinets. Then the British realised it would effectively guarantee France, with whom negotiations had stalled, and so it fell victim to the clashing mentalities and aims of Lloyd George and Poincaré. Only the Locarno Treaty in October 1925, in whose negotiation Hymans participated in the early phases, brought Belgium two dubious benefits. Its preamble included the clause: 'Taking note of the abrogation of the treaties for the neutralisation of Belgium',[15] though that neutrality had never been formally abrogated. The Treaty itself brought the long-sought British guarantee, along with that of Italy, but it was inoperable. Modern warfare required advance arrangements. Inasmuch as Britain had guaranteed both sides, it had to engage in staff talks with France and Belgium on the one hand and with Germany on the other, or with neither. It chose to avoid staff talks altogether, leaving an empty promise as it briefly attained the centre of the balance of power.

For Belgium, the search for security had been long, painful, and largely futile. Its geography and the attitudes of its stronger neighbours determined its circumstances. Aside from the unpopular Franco-Belgian accord and the pointless abortive Anglo-French interim guarantee, everything it gained or sought was a sideline to some Great Power arrangement, whether the Anglo-American guarantee of France, the abortive Anglo-French treaty, initiatives at the League of Nations, or the Locarno Pact. Hymans did not always see that power was needed to enforce Belgium's 'rights', which were more often desires than rights. In reviewing the outcome of the peace negotiations, Count Charles Woeste, a Catholic elder statesman, remarked: 'We are under the control of a sort of superior power [*force majeure*].' [16] In truth, that had been Belgium's problem from the outset.

9
The Hinge of the Entente

During the Peace Conference, Hymans sought Belgian participation in the ongoing entities being created to supervise the Versailles Treaty whenever they dealt with Belgian interests. As he later said: *Peace has been decreed; it has not been made. The Supreme Council, the Reparations Commission, the Conference of Ambassadors continue to discuss and try to solidify the most important clauses of the Versailles Treaty.*[1] In this matter, if not others, Hymans was successful, with results exceeding anyone's expectations. Little Belgium, insulated before the war and isolated during it, suddenly found itself at centre stage in the diplomatic limelight, consorting with Europe's Great Powers and providing a much-needed hinge to the Western Entente trying to deal with Germany. As the Peace Conference had been a Great Power conclave, it was assumed that further meetings would be as well, and the new Belgian role, which continued through the 1920s, was unanticipated.

Belgium's prominence owed something to its own efforts and more to the impossibility of excluding it. As Jaspar said: 'Belgium is not, in Europe, an out-of-the-way corner of land, whose scanty territory renders her negligible; she is an essential factor in the solution of many problems.' [2] For this reason, as the United States failed to ratify the Treaty and retired to observer status, the Big Four became the Three and a Half. This did not simply happen; an early Great Power session in March 1920 illustrates Jaspar's remark. As Germany sought permission to send troops into the Ruhr, which abutted the Belgian Rhineland zone, there could be no serious opposition to Belgium joining in the decision. The same was true with questions about the Rhineland, war crimes trials, reparations or potential punitive action against Germany, which arose often.

Belgium's role in the Western Entente was foreshadowed by its membership on so many Peace Conference Commissions, indicating its involvement with much of the settlement. Moreover, the Treaty granted membership in two key agencies. As an occupying state, Belgium held a seat on the Inter-Allied Rhineland High Commission which administered the occupation and dealt with German civil authorities, who continued to function. Though the United States kept a small military contingent in the Rhineland until January 1923, it did not take up its seat, leaving Britain, France and Belgium, the latter in theory decisive. During the 1923 Ruhr occupation, France and Belgium registered ordinances at will; Britain, which opposed the occupation, merely abstained.

In addition, Belgium was a member of the new Reparations Commission for all German matters except naval ones. It was to be a five-state Commission chaired by the United States, the least interested member, wherein to avoid potential deadlock (a two-two vote) abstention would count as a negative vote. Upon American departure, France, the most interested party, claimed both the chair and the second, casting vote granted chairmen of other committees in case of a tie. Though never used on a German question, its existence in reserve meant France could control the Commission with one other member. As Britain and France rarely agreed, and Italy usually opted for the stronger side, Belgium could determine which that was, a situation fully appreciated by France and ignored by Britain.

There remained the new Conference of Ambassadors in Paris, charged with completing leftover matters from the Versailles Treaty, and the Great Power gatherings. Hymans campaigned from late 1919 through March 1920 to ensure Belgian participation in both. The Powers soon decided the Belgian envoy could join the Conference of Ambassadors for German matters, which in practice meant whenever somebody remembered to invite him, but his presence became a habit. The same was true in the Inter-Allied Military Committee at Versailles. Belgium did not participate in the Military Control Commissions attempting to supervise German disarmament because the Treaty specified Allied Great Powers only, but its presence in the Military Committee, the Conference of Ambassadors and ultimately Supreme Councils provided a voice on disarmament policy.

Entrance into Supreme Councils was more difficult. The term, used in the war and also at the Peace Conference for the Councils of Ten and Four, denoted meetings of heads of governments, presumably Great Powers; eventually such gatherings simply were called conferences. One Supreme Council in December 1919 and two in January 1920 occurred without Hymans, as then and thereafter did brief Anglo-French meetings. But German questions requiring Belgian attendance arose at London meetings in February and March 1920. Thereafter, as attention turned to Eastern and Middle

Eastern topics, its presence was questioned, but, despite frequent British objections, Hymans sought to attend on the well-founded assumption that questions would arise about German reparations. He was at the San Remo Conference in April, which decided that the next large conference – the first with German participation – would be at Spa in Belgium and attended another in June at Boulogne which addressed German disarmament, reparations and plans for Spa. Belgium was becoming a fixture.

Hymans and his successors adapted with astonishing ease to their new prominence. To a man, they sought compromise, Entente unity and maximum reparations. Belgium had no guarantee and no proper European balance of power to protect it. It hoped to lean on Britain and France against Germany and to balance between the two faithful Guarantors to gain some freedom of action. But Britain and France rarely agreed, and Italy rarely cared. When Britain and France managed to decide on action against Germany, Belgium made a substantial contribution, usually more than Britain. In general, it would accept anything the two senior partners decided if neither priority nor privilege were affected. It tried to avoid unattractive choices, seeking both redemption of occupation marks and extradition of alleged war criminals, thus gaining neither. The rift in the Entente became so acute that Belgian leaders literally trudged back and forth between the hotel rooms of senior partners who were not speaking to each other, earnestly devising compromises to paper over the divide. Their solutions usually gave France the form and Britain the substance, but earned no gratitude from the latter, which always assumed Belgium to be a French satellite, though that was only occasionally true.

The underlying problem was differing assessments of the

power balance. For Britain, France was the traditional foe and the only Power close enough to bomb England. Lloyd George, who remained in office until October 1922, became steadily more hostile to France, whose power he greatly exaggerated, and more determined to build up Germany, whose weakness he erroneously assumed was permanent, to counter French 'dominance'. He was also allergic to everything Belgian, including the climate, the cuisine and the central heating, and feared a Russo-German combination, which emerged to a degree. He knew but did not understand French fear of a more populous, younger Germany, stronger in the long run, and the desire of every French Premier to cling to Britain for protection. France wished to enforce key Treaty clauses, Lloyd George (who soon consorted with the Germans behind French backs) to revise the Treaty piecemeal to German benefit, which did not satisfy a Germany seeking dramatic renunciation but meanwhile engaging in 'the continuation of war by another means'.[3] At Supreme Councils, Britain and France often both demanded Belgian compliance with their conflicting orders and that Belgium arrange the compliance of the other. Belgian compromises frequently evoked the wrath of both.

Belgian leaders were proud of their thankless role, effectively that of satellite to a bloc, which gave them more prominence than security or freedom of action but at least placated the Flemings and limited French domination. They defined their role as that of a hyphen. One scholar adds: 'Belgium, like a hyphen, did not carry enough weight to claim a diplomatic identity of her own.'[4] Belgians made the most of what they had, working through conference after conference to solidify the peace and enhance Belgian economic and political security and managing to avoid a choice of partner and paper over the rift until 1923. Whether an earlier break-down of the Entente would have been wiser is unclear, but in any event Hymans and his successors were hardworking and well-intentioned.

The nature of relationships within the Western Entente was such that the hosts for the Spa Conference had difficulty in learning the date, agenda and guest list. At Boulogne, the Allies agreed to meet ahead at Brussels to ensure a united front against Germany. On 1 July 1920, delegates and experts arrived to find that a strike of rail employees, including porters, forced them to trundle their luggage on handcarts through the streets of Brussels to their hotels. The formal sessions on 2 and 3 July were less important than unofficial ones in Lloyd George's hotel rooms. These dealt primarily with allocation of reparations receipts when they became available. Lloyd George adamantly objected to eight per cent for Belgium, causing the matter to be carried over to Spa, to which the Conference adjourned on 4 July. Belgium gained eight per cent at the price of some alteration of its priority to the benefit of other reparations-hungry powers. The route to Brussels and Spa did not traverse the devastated areas, confirming Lloyd George's misconception of Belgian circum-stances. A friend noted in his diary: 'L. G. much impressed by Belgian prosperity. He describes the Belgians as, per head, the richest nation in Europe.'[5]

At Spa, delegations were housed in chateaux and villas lent by wealthy Belgians – the French in the wartime residence of the Kaiser. By intent to avoid incidents with bitter citizens, the German delegation was placed in an inn outside the town amid fields and woods. Delacroix presided, firmly suppress-ing the German industrialist Hugo Stinnes, who complained of those 'afflicted with the disease of victory'.[6] Despite another eruption, the Germans were invited to tea with the Allies (though dining together had to await Locarno). The Conference, which lasted until 16 July, had a varied agenda including trials of war criminals, Czech and Polish questions, and the Treaty of Sèvres.

Primarily, however, Spa focused on the main battlegrounds with Germany, disarmament and reparations, notably defaults on coal deliveries. Under threats (which Lloyd George had no intention of making good), Germany bowed to the Entente on both. Before that happened, however, came the first of several Allied discussions of an occupation of the Ruhr as the obvious sanction if coercion were necessary. The Belgians backed British reluctance, stressing the difficulties. Delacroix, Jaspar and Theunis handled reparations, disarmament and defence of Belgian priority, which other states endorsed in principle but sought to circumvent in practice, especially as German payments proved to be very slow. Hymans made a final effort to gain British participation in the Franco-Belgian military accord and dealt with Luxembourg.

After Spa, intense Anglo-French disagreement prevented further Supreme Councils in 1920. In late August, Hymans resigned. He returned to practicing law, remained a deputy, and was active at the League of Nations. Within months there was a new Belgian team. Theunis, as Finance Minister and Prime Minister, and Jaspar as Foreign Minister took on the task of trying to introduce enough flexibility into the Western Entente so that Britain and France could bend toward each other. Jaspar's explosive temper never appeared on the international scene where he added useful jests, whereas Theunis's modesty for himself and his country, genuine comprehension of intricate reparations plans and ability to translate fuzzy notions into workable schemes rendered him invaluable.

Unfortunately, Lloyd George came to appreciate the utility of the Belgian team only just before he left office.

By then, their task was becoming impossible. When in January 1923 Britain insisted on a reparations plan politically suicidal for all Continental recipients and frontally assaulting Belgian priority, they reluctantly joined Poincaré's encirclement of the Ruhr and occupation of Essen to collect coal and salvage the Versailles Treaty despite British disapproval. As Poincaré froze into immobility, they urged stiffer action to shorten the ordeal, then pressured him to make decisions, and finally in September 1923 earned his wrath by trying to ease the surrender of the new German Chancellor, Gustav Stresemann. Thereupon they reverted at once to their prior middle role, doing all in their limited power to restore the Entente and Europe. Charged by Britain with obtaining French acceptance of one of two plans to resolve the crisis, they gained Poincaré's consent to the lesser one, an expert committee to examine the situation, thereby incurring Curzon's fury because they had not achieved the impossible broader plan.

Jaspar resigned in late February 1924 when the Chamber rejected the economic treaty he had finally achieved with France in May 1923 in the context of the Ruhr occupation. In March, Hymans succeeded him in a new Theunis Cabinet with a stronger Flemish element and an even greater desire to end the Ruhr venture. Theunis was not pleased to have Hymans, but they learned to work together. As Hymans could not possibly master the intricacies of three and a half years of reparations politics during his absence from office, Theunis took sole charge of this topic whereas Hymans dealt with other aspects of the Ruhr situation. Their task was eased but complicated by Anglo-French changes as well. In January the leader of the Labour Party, Ramsay MacDonald, had become Britain's Prime Minister and Foreign Minister, substituting amiability for Curzon's irascibility. In June, Poincaré fell, a victim of tax increases, and was replaced by Édouard Herriot, a Radical Socialist (i.e. centrist) who wanted good relations with Belgium. Neither state's policy shifted much, but the tone improved.

Hymans characterised the period of his absence from office as *three years of international difficulties, of political and economic complications produced by the reparations problem which led to the Ruhr occupation, then to the search for a practical compromise solution.*[8] The new Cabinet, aware that the Ruhr venture had confirmed assumptions about Belgian sub-

> Belgium's role will depend, as always, to a great extent on the worth of her experts.
> PAUL HYMANS[7]

servience to France, was eager to both demonstrate independence and hasten that compromise solution which would entail a new reparations scheme as well as military and economic evacuations of the Ruhr. In April 1924 the expert committee, presided over by American General Charles Dawes, produced a reparations plan which no state liked but all approved for lack of another. Its ambiguous political clauses were the work of American Owen D Young, but its technical aspects were a compromise between the views of Sir Josiah Stamp of Britain and Belgium's Emile Francqui, whose contributions included the new supervisory structure to be created in Berlin.

To speed implementation of the Dawes Plan, Theunis and Hymans visited Paris in Poincaré's last days and then saw MacDonald, gaining little. The Italian Prime Minister Benito Mussolini threatened to feel slighted, so they obligingly went to Milan. Once in office, Herriot, who was inexperienced, naïve and disorganised, rushed to see MacDonald but punctiliously offered to visit Brussels before he went and afterwards as well. The Belgian Cabinet decided to decline consultation to demonstrate independence, but Hymans had already arranged to see Herriot briefly 'between trains'[9] en route home from the League of Nations. When Herriot visited after seeing MacDonald, the more experienced Belgians were not impressed. Theunis said: 'He is a child.'[10]

The Allied Powers met on 16 July for the month-long London Conference to implement the Dawes Plan as a major revision of the Versailles Treaty's reparations clauses and to devise an end to the Ruhr occupation. Hymans, who was eager to leave the Ruhr and not irritate Germany unnecessarily, told the Chamber that *it was impossible to let the occasion pass, perhaps the last, to resolve a problem which weighs so heavily on the European economy.*[11] At London, he worked on the military evacuation, a potential Belgian-German trade treaty since the Versailles Treaty's five-year economic clauses would soon expire, and plans to make declaration of German reparations default more difficult, including adding an American citizen to the Reparations Committee for such occasions, as was done.

Emile Francqui (1863–1935), a financier and statesman, spent his early career in the Congo and China. During the First World War, he supervised the National Committee of Aid and Alimentation. A 'King's man', he became a director of the vast Société Générale de Belgique in 1912, and Vice-Governor then Governor in 1932. He worked on the mark question and reparations through the 1920s, serving on both the Dawes and Young Committees, and contributing to creation of the Bank of International Settlements. A Minister of State from 1918, he served as Minister without Portfolio in 1926 to stabilise the Belgian franc and again in 1934–5. Nominally a Liberal, he was a friend of Jaspar, Delacroix and Vandervelde. (See *Emile Francqui ou l'intelligence créatrice* by Liane Ranieri.)

The Paul Hymans at London was very different from the 'pestiferous mosquito' of Paris five years before. Though the Foreign Office still disliked him and an official there called him a windbag 'who never ceases to blow',[12] he said little in the morning meetings of delegation leaders. No longer obsessively precise, when others haggled over details he facilitated progress by reminding that the Conference *could not provide ... for every contingency which might arise*,[13] and, as some pressed for speedier evacuation than French politics could accept, noted that *not everything can change from one day to the next. We need time*[14] but urged compromise. After the German Chancellor Wilhelm Marx and Stresemann, now Foreign Minister, arrived on 5 August, the Belgians were largely ignored, though still at the morning meetings. At one, Philip Snowden, Chancellor of the Exchequer, who supported Germany so ardently as to alarm even Stresemann, began 'My chief point is ...' and Hymans finished in a stage whisper, *to stand always on the side of the German delegation.*[15] As the Conference reached its crisis, Hymans gained most of his information from the press, but remained patiently stoic. He erupted only once – by pre-arrangement with Theunis to display their anger with Herriot, who, under domestic political pressure and the stress of an intense conference, had become rather frantic and had announced concessions involving Belgium without consulting or even informing them. Among other decisions, he agreed to immediate evacuation of Ruhrort, the transportation and logistics hub of the Belgian zone, a promise he had to retract. Aside from that, Belgium did not object to the substance of the decisions, only the lack of consultation.

On 16 August documents were signed assuring an immediate end to the economic occupation and to the military occupation within a year, an international loan to Germany, a reduced schedule of reparations payments rising gradually, a new supervisory structure in Berlin headed by an American Agent-General for Reparations to bypass the Reparations Commission, and new procedures in the latter for default declarations. The Versailles Treaty had been significantly revised. When Stresemann, as part of his effort at financial stabilisation, sought to introduce his new interim currency in the Rhineland, Britain and Belgium assented, to French fury. Thereafter, Allied Finance Ministers wrestled with the complicated Ruhr receipts. Belgium again successfully defended its priority, demonstrating that it was not yet extinct and agreeing that upon extinction (before 1 September 1926), it would 'repay' the priority by a reduction of its reparations percentage to 4.5 per cent.

At London, it was also agreed among the Entente that the first or Cologne Rhineland zone (which included the entire British sector, much of the Belgian sector and part of the French sector) would not be evacuated until a new disarmament inspection was completed. When that showed considerable violation of Treaty requirements, Belgium supported Britain's desire merely to summarise, not enumerate, defaults in the note to Germany stating that evacuation would not occur on 10 January 1925, as scheduled. By then, MacDonald had been replaced by Stanley Baldwin as Prime Minister and Austen Chamberlain as Foreign Secretary. Hymans wasted no time in proposing a British-Belgian alliance. The Francophile Chamberlain aspired to a tripartite alliance with France and Belgium to ease French fears, but in March 1925 the British Cabinet opted instead to pursue Stresemann's offer of a Rhineland pact. This was designed to achieve evacuation of the Cologne zone without further disarmament and to avert a tripartite Entente treaty, in which it succeeded.

Stresemann's initial proposal contained no mention of Belgium. That was no accident, for he intended to begin territorial revision at the weakest point facing Germany. But Britain and France quickly ensured Belgian inclusion. Like the French, Hymans would have preferred a tripartite treaty but would accept a Rhenish pact to gain the projected British guarantee. From Geneva, he reported: *I think the moment is favourable for a diplomatic action able to achieve an accord between England, France, and Belgium, to which Germany would adhere.*[16] Hymans was involved in the early negotiations which culminated at Locarno, but elections at the start of April set off a long political crisis, matched by political and/or diplomatic changes in other countries, causing a hiatus. He acted as Foreign Minister until mid-May and at League meetings in June discussed the pact proposal with Chamberlain and Aristide Briand, who had just become French Foreign Minister.

When negotiations resumed in June, Vandervelde was the Belgian Foreign Minister. It was he who ensured that the phrasing of the Anglo-Italian guarantee in the eventual treaty specified 'the inviolability of the said frontiers as fixed by or in pursuance of the Treaty of Peace …'[17] to cover Eupen and Malmédy. Unlike the Czech and Polish Foreign Ministers, he attended the entire Conference but was more informed than consulted. When Briand, Chamberlain and Stresemann went boating on Lake Maggiore and returned with the 'texte de bateau'[18] ('boat text') to exempt Germany from any League military sanctions, he queried, in a classic small-state expression of concern for the League's enforcement powers, whether the text did not (as indeed it did) make all sanctions, economic and military, optional for all states, and was squelched by the senior partners.

After the Locarno signing ceremonies in London in December 1925, where additional business was conducted, there were no major conferences for several years. In part, with reparations temporarily settled, disarmament inspections ending and evacuation of the Cologne zone in January 1926 as a by-product of Locarno, there were fewer occasions where Germany asked and the Entente had to answer in unison. Also, Germany joined the League of Nations as a permanent Council member in September 1926 just as Belgium's six years on the Council ended, owing to a new rule of rotation for non-permanent members. Great Power foreign ministers now usually attended the quarterly Council sessions, and so they met together regularly in their hotel rooms to settle Europe's business, making Geneva, if not the League of Nations, the new centre of European diplomacy[19] to the dismay of smaller states not included in these 'Locarno tea-parties'. Belgium participated mainly for German questions, and its role became somewhat less prominent.

In May 1926 Hymans returned to the Cabinet as Minister of Justice, an office he held for a year and a half but scarcely mentioned in his memoirs. Cabinet membership, however, and trips to Geneva through September afforded some entrée into foreign affairs. In November 1927 he again became Foreign Minister and remained so until mid-1934, participating in the quieter diplomacy of the late 1920s. He favoured concessions on reparations to Stresemann so the right wing would not gain control in Germany and also sought greater independence from France.

1928 was marked by leisurely negotiation of what became the toothless Kellogg-Briand Peace Pact. The United States consulted Hymans and invited him to be among the 15 original signatories on 27 August. Although ill, Stresemann came as well, the first German Foreign Minister to visit Paris since 1871. While there, as expected, he sought downward revision of reparations, whose annual payments under the Dawes Plan were becoming substantial, and early evacuation of the Rhineland.

These requests had been signaled in advance. The Agent-General for Reparations urged revision, and both Poincaré, again premier, and Hymans favoured evacuating while one could still gain something for doing so. The Belgian Cabinet had considered the issue. The third zone was of no interest but the second zone, which covered Liège, mattered to Belgium. Nonetheless, it could not oppose Britain and France, and evacuation of the second zone, scheduled for 1930, would be only slightly early. Hymans was also willing to re-examine reparations if Belgium gained a settlement regarding the occupation marks, which mattered to him personally as much as to Francqui.

> It would not be good policy to prolong the occupation uselessly until 1935.
>
> PAUL HYMANS[20]

From Paris, most of the statesmen proceeded to Geneva for a League Assembly session. A series of Entente 'tea-parties' without Stresemann but including Hymans issued the 'Geneva communiqué'[21] on 16 September calling for a new reparations plan and reconsideration of the Rhineland occupation. The new expert committee was led by Owen D Young and included Francqui, who flatly refused to sign the resultant plan until a marks agreement was achieved. He gained a fairly generous scheme which provided useful revenue for several years until Adolf Hitler put an end to it.

The Young Plan linked reparations to Allied war debt payments to the United States by spreading them over 62 years.

German payments for the first ten years were to be low, implying future reduction. In addition, only about a third of each
annuity was unconditionally payable, the remainder being
postponable in times of economic distress. Belgium reverted
to eight per cent but only in conditional payments. The Dawes
supervisory structure and the Reparations Commission would
both end; instead, a new Bank of International Settlements
would receive and distribute reparations receipts and provide a
link among central banks. In its latter function, it still survives.

To put the Young Plan into effect, two conferences were
held at The Hague, the first throughout August 1929. Jaspar,
then Prime Minister, presided at both, whereas Hymans,
as Belgian delegate, had an active role, especially as to the
Rhineland evacuation. A phased evacuation was established,
ending nearly five years ahead of schedule on 30 June 1930.
Reaching agreement took so long that the delegates had to
proceed onward to Geneva for League meetings. Thus business was left unfinished, and a second session was held in
January 1930 to settle East European reparations and complete the reparations and Rhineland settlement.

With the Young Plan and the Rhineland evacuation, Belgium's decade in the limelight ended, and it opted for a more
modest role. Its efforts to bring its senior partners together
had produced intermittent successes on specific issues but no
real meeting of the minds in the Western Entente, which, in
any event, would have ended the Belgian role. The diplomacy
of the 1920s gave Belgium prominence but not much freedom
of action or security. The experience, however, altered and
matured Belgian diplomacy as its leaders learned much and
accepted more. Hymans in particular came to understand
and, more importantly, to accept the limitations on the role
of a small state.

10

The Post-War Decade

The efforts of Hymans to gain entry into the Western Entente and then to keep it functioning were time-consuming but only a portion of his duties. He had a key ministry to run and did so well. He had a party to lead as domestic politics continued unabated and did that without challenge. Like other Cabinet members, he was concerned with the economic, physical and psychological reconstruction of Belgium. Several distinctly Belgian foreign policy issues kept recurring. Beyond all that, he chose to take on another difficult, time-consuming task. Paul Hymans was deeply involved with the League of Nations most of the time from early 1920 into 1935. He was very much one of the 'men of Geneva' and, according to Anthony Eden, became 'respected and much loved'.[1]

Why he invested so much time and energy in the League is not clear. Granted, the small states, who were far more enthusiastic about collective security than the Great Powers which would have to provide it, sent senior statesmen to League meetings from the outset whereas Europe's leading states did so routinely only after 1925. Hymans, however, never considered the League to be the solution to Belgium's security problem. His comment on the Geneva Protocol of 1924 that it was acceptable as a *roof* but that solid pillars of *regional ententes* were needed as well could stand as his view of the League in general.[2] He favoured collective security, mediation, arbitration and efforts at conciliation, of which he made many, but not what he deemed premature disarmament, and he was realistic enough to know in 1919 that no League police force was likely, given Anglo-American opposition, and that little international spirit yet existed in the aftermath of a bitter war.

Hymans also understood the League's proper role. In 1921 he said that while some laughed, *it is an authority which has come into the world and which is trying to find itself and its role. The establishment of a world public opinion, given its instruments, its leverage, its means of action, will alter the appearance and the proceedings of international politics ... . the Assembly of the League of Nations may become, if trust surrounds and endorses it, not the super-parliament of a super-state, but the moral arbiter.*[4]

Will the League of Nations save this ancient world? Possibly. That is only a hope.

PAUL HYMANS[3]

He consistently supported the small states and, as they wished, fought for the League's competence in disputes and for application of its rules. He became known for his efficiency, organising skills and fairness. Like Briand, he could be relied on to provide a suitable address for any occasion and his oratorical skills were on full display at Geneva.

In addition to a great deal of work, the League gave Hymans a wider stage where he was often in the spotlight and the headlines. Possibly this suited his ego, though more likely he was honest in saying he believed in moral force and the power of ideas as well as progress and thought something of value was slowly being constructed. Curiously, though, aside from a section on the Disarmament Conference of the 1930s and reports of negotiations with individual statesmen on non-League matters, his memoirs ignore his activities there. In any event, his efforts gave him prominence, a little influence and almost no power. It is unlikely that he would have invested so much energy if he had not thought the League worthwhile, but probably its greatest single attraction for him was that it enabled him to remain involved in Belgium's foreign affairs when he was out of office altogether or not Foreign Minister. No Belgian Cabinet could permit him to attend Council and Assembly meetings, where he would meet other Foreign Ministers including the Dutch one, without thorough briefings on all current issues. And as the years went by, more and more diplomatic questions which had little or nothing to do with the League were negotiated during but outside its sessions which provided the convenient diplomatic gatherings that state funerals have more recently offered.

If this was a key motive, it probably appeared very early. Hymans was appointed by the Council as Acting President of the first Assembly and then immediately elected to that position just after he had resigned the Foreign Ministry. In August 1920, while Hymans was absent at a League Council meeting, the Cabinet refused to permit shipment of arms from France via Antwerp to Polish forces defending Warsaw against Bolshevik attack. On his return, he sought but failed to gain its reversal. It is unclear whether Hymans resigned because he felt strongly about the issue or, knowing the Cabinet would resign soon in any event, to avoid a difficult vote on a language question. Either way, most of his early League career occurred while out of office.

He was already an experienced League hand. The Versailles Treaty (Article 4) specified that the Assembly would elect the small state members of the Council but that, until it did so, Belgium, Brazil, Greece and Spain would sit. The Council first met in January 1920 and became a travelling troupe until quarters in Geneva were found, holding eight meetings in ten months as it sought to organise itself and the Secretariat, and arriving in Geneva just before the first Assembly meeting in November. The Council feared this larger assemblage might be unruly, and so put Hymans in charge temporarily. His opening address attested to the aspirations of peoples for a peaceful organisation of international relations. He faced a vast agenda and much organising to supervise, which he did well.

Even before this, the Council had given Hymans the difficult job of arbitrating the bitter Polish-Lithuanian dispute over Vilna (Wilno, Vilnius). An initial agreement was voided by Polish seizure of Vilna. Thereafter, Hymans spent ten months devising ingenious scheme after scheme for both sides to reject. In January 1922, he and the Council conceded defeat and Poland kept Vilna. However, the experience established his reputation as an arbiter. Thus he presided over committees engaged in arbitrating a dispute between Finland and Norway and another between Switzerland and Romania. Meanwhile, the Council had assigned the plebiscite which the Versailles Treaty (Article 88) specified for Upper Silesia and the difficult partition thereafter to its four small power members (including China, which had replaced Greece) whose states were in no way involved in the problem. Hymans presided actively over their labours. His solution, which he carefully cleared with Britain and France, gave Poland more voters than it otherwise might have had but also returned a key city to Germany. Berlin's anger affected Belgian-German relations, but his plan was adopted.

In 1922 Hymans served as President of the Council. As early as the Peace Conference, he had sought to establish a League Committee on Intellectual Relations. In 1922 the Council appointed a committee of eminent persons including Albert Einstein, Marie Curie, Gilbert Murray and Henri Bergson. The goals were to improve the conditions of intellectual workers, worsened by the war; to create international contacts among teachers, artists, scientists, authors and such-like (which two Belgians had been attempting on a small scale); and to strengthen the League's influence for peace, especially through teachers and professors. The Committee planned a modest agenda, including investigating dire conditions for intellectual workers in Eastern Europe, but was starved for funds. In 1924 France offered to establish an Institute of Intellectual Cooperation in Paris under the League committee. It started slowly, but a second Institute was created in Rome, also under the League. These entities and the committee, founded largely at the initiative of Hymans and the two other Belgians, were the seeds of UNESCO and made some progress until intense nationalism prevented harmony.

Meanwhile, in 1923 Hymans joined with representatives of other small states in a vain effort to prevent removal of the Corfu crisis between Italy and Greece (wherein Mussolini seized Corfu from Greece after the Italian member of the boundary commission delimiting the Graeco-Albanian frontier was mysteriously murdered on Greek soil) from the competence of the Council, learning once again that rules did not apply to Great Powers. On the other hand, he supported French determination to block a Swedish effort to put the Ruhr occupation on the Council agenda. Thus the League heard nothing of Europe's greatest crisis that year. Hymans was as unenthusiastic as most others about the 1922–3 Draft Treaty of Mutual Assistance, aimed at providing security to enable disarmament. He liked the Geneva Protocol, which linked arbitration, security and disarmament, the next year somewhat better but wasted no time upon Austen Chamberlain's accession to office in renewing his efforts toward a Belgian-British treaty.

It was awkward that Belgium left the Council just as Germany joined it. One French diplomat said it was scandalous to give Germany 'the seat of Belgium, the victim, whom the League of Nations dismisses, in order to install there its tormentor'.[5] but Belgium accepted with good grace what was largely an accident of timing. Hymans remained a member of the Assembly and attended the more important Locarno tea-parties, including the one in 1928 which issued the Geneva communiqué leading to the Young Plan and The Hague conferences.

When Europe's statesmen moved *en masse* from the first Hague Conference to Geneva, Hymans pleaded on 5 September 1929 at the tenth Assembly for 'economic disarmament',[6] meaning a gradual progressive reduction of tariffs. Briand seized on the phrase and launched his famous plea for European economic union, which, upon inspection, proved to be more political than economic. On this optimistic note, the League's decade ended, though Hymans' labours there continued onward into a darker time.

His early years at the League brought him into frequent contact with Herman van Karnebeek, the longtime Dutch Foreign Minister, who succeeded him (with the endorsement of Hymans) as President of the Assembly. Gradually, the two men came to know and like each other, which would not have occurred before the League provided a frequent meeting-place. When Hymans returned to the Foreign Ministry in 1924, he took advantage of the fact that he and van Karnebeek were staying in the same Geneva hotel to initiate quiet conversations about the 1839 Belgian-Dutch Treaty. As a result a new Belgian-Dutch Treaty not differing greatly from the 1920 version was signed at The Hague on 3 April 1925. Belgian-Dutch relations improved immediately, but Hymans did not benefit since elections forced the entire Theunis Cabinet out of office.

The two signatories jointly sought a second treaty from the Great Powers dealing with Belgium's international status and abrogating the 1839 Collective Treaty. In London, the Foreign Office contemplated linking such a document to the Rhineland pact then under negotiation. Though this was not done, the phrase taking note of the abrogation of Belgian neutrality crept into the Locarno Treaty's text. After some startling efforts by Britain and France to gain or retain control of Belgium's international status indefinitely and even of details of navigation on the Scheldt, causing an eruption in previously unheard-of unison from Belgium and Holland, a collective treaty specifically contingent upon the Belgian-Dutch treaty was signed on 27 May 1926, although dated 22 May. The Soviet Union was invited to adhere, though informed that recognition was not thereby granted. The Belgian Parliament approved the Belgian-Dutch Treaty overwhelmingly, but Rotterdam shipping interests were hostile, opposing concessions to rival Antwerp. During an intense press campaign, the 1925 Treaty scraped through the Second Chamber of the Dutch Estates General but was emphatically rejected by the First Chamber. Thus both Treaties lapsed.

Another attempt in 1928 failed after the Dutch press

published two forged documents, one allegedly the Franco-Belgian military accord, implying Belgian designs on Dutch territory and leading Holland to try to insist on Belgian neutrality. In August 1929, during the first Hague Conference, the Dutch proposed another attempt. This time, trusted non-diplomatic persons (with experts) were to negotiate in secret unofficially outside both countries with governments informed but not involved. Talks went well, but the Dutch suddenly wanted prompt settlement before their election season opened. In the final weeks of negotiation, two or three key points could not be resolved and Hymans gathered that the Dutch Cabinet no longer sought a settlement. None eventuated, then or thereafter. A Dutch diplomatic note in 1933 recognised that Belgian neutrality had lapsed. Aside from the preamble to the Locarno Treaty, this remained the only inter-war recognition that Belgium was no longer in a state of obligatory neutrality.

The intent of the Locarno Pact was to freeze the Franco-German and Belgian-German frontiers in perpetuity. However, a few days after the euphoric closing ceremony in October 1925, Stresemann took advantage of a certain German-induced murkiness in the text to argue that the Treaty only ruled out frontier alteration by force, an interpretation no other Power endorsed; he did so in order to seek retrocession of Eupen and Malmédy in return for a financial settlement for the German occupation marks still held by the Belgian National Bank. He had tried earlier in the spring of 1925 while his Rhenish proposal was under negotiation. Belgium rejected both approaches. From this point on, the Eupen-Malmédy question was inextricably attached to that of the six milliard occupation marks (seven and a half milliard Belgian francs) and both became entangled with wider

European issues, as the marks question had been throughout the decade. An initial settlement in late 1919 was rejected by Germany because Belgium did not altogether abandon extradition of alleged war criminals; though it reduced its list sharply, it indicated it would accept a Great Power decision on trials, thereby declining to serve as Germany's entering wedge. Another agreement on 1 September 1921 was held up by the Berlin Cabinet because the League committee led by Hymans did not award all of Upper Silesia to Germany. Further negotiations were unsuccessful. Germany raised the matter again during the 1923 Ruhr occupation, hoping to tempt Belgium to abandon France. Eager as Belgium was for the ordeal to end, it rejected the overture.

In 1926 the questions of Eupen-Malmédy and of the marks became a major issue both within Belgium and internationally. In March, Belgium went into acute financial crisis as domestic and foreign debt was excessive, the franc depreciated rapidly and most reparations received under the Dawes Plan went to pay the American debt. As panic developed, a three-party Cabinet was formed in May with Francqui the dominant figure as Minister without Portfolio charged to solve the crisis. As early as April, Stresemann proposed linking Eupen-Malmédy and the marks issue without effect, but talks continued with Delacroix, then part of the Dawes supervisory structure in Berlin. Finally, Germany, which seemed to have funds for what it wanted, offered $20 million cash plus $30 million in an interest free brief loan repayable in 30 monthly installments by deduction from the Belgian share of the Dawes annuities in return for retrocession of the two cantons.

The matter went before the Belgian Cabinet in July in the absence of Hymans in the Chamber. It had been seeking better relations with Germany since Locarno, and an active minority of the public, comprised of financiers and socialists, favoured return of the cantons, though the majority did not. In the Cabinet, Francqui, whose preoccupation was exclusively financial, strongly favoured accepting the offer. Vandervelde as Foreign Minister cautiously agreed, while Prime Minister Jaspar was hesitant. Upon his return, Hymans objected emphatically, pointing out the political implications, arguing that retrocession would amount to a major German victory regarding the Versailles Treaty and threatening resignation. As opinion was divided, the Cabinet decided to consult France and Britain. Briand was willing, but Poincaré, who had just become Premier again, was adamantly opposed, as were the British, both fearing a precedent for other borders. Thus Belgium rejected the German offer in August and quickly stabilised its currency by other means.

In September, Germany entered the League of Nations as a permanent Council member, as projected at Locarno. A week later, Briand and Stresemann met for a long lunch at a country inn at Thoiry in Switzerland. Authorship of the plan they discussed is in dispute, but in essence Stresemann hoped to use crises of the French franc, the Belgian franc and the Polish zloty to buy his way out of many Versailles Treaty territorial and Rhenish clauses, including those about Eupen-Malmédy. As the scheme faced many objections, including some German second thoughts, it never materialised. Belgium, which had not been consulted or informed by Briand, joined Britain in opposition.

In October 1926, Stresemann tried again to arrange retrocession of the cantons for redemption of the marks, to no avail. Another approach in September 1927 led Vandervelde to say that both questions should be discussed in relation to an early evacuation of the Rhineland, which was already in the air. In November, Hymans became Foreign Minister, and Belgium considered the matter closed. There were no further overtures until the Young Plan to reduce reparations again was being negotiated. Strese-mann preferred not to mix ter-ritorial issues with negotiations over reparations and ending the Rhineland occupation, but

> At The Hague there was an air of pacification and hope.
>
> PAUL HYMANS[7]

others sought Eupen-Malmédy. This led to a stalemate jeopardising reparations revision. The United States intervened and gained a German guarantee that no territorial questions would be raised. This ended the Eupen-Malmédy question until the Second World War.

There remained the issue of the occupation marks. Francqui's insistence was supported by Young and the Agent-General for Reparations. Thus Germany had to commit to negotiating a settlement with Belgium and to accept that the Young Plan would not enter into force until a binding agreement existed about the marks. The result was a Belgian-German treaty in July 1929 affording Belgium 37 annuities in varying amounts which, in effect, increased Belgium's yield from the new plan until May 1934 while that of other states was reduced.

The Conference held at The Hague to put all these arrangements into effect, consisting in its August 1929 session of five Great Powers and Belgium, was grandly titled 'Conference on the Final Liquidation of the War', meaning in practice liquidation of the Peace Settlement. The Conference included a 'Committee on the Liquidation of the Past' reflecting a widespread desire to move on. Hymans said: *The Hague Conference was the result of a policy of conciliation and reconciliation which the English on one hand and Briand on the other had pursued since the Dawes Plan and the evacuation of the Ruhr.*[8] Although, as at Locarno, harmony was more apparent than real, Europe had moved a considerable distance toward pacification, in which Hymans had done his modest part, and Belgium seemed somewhat more secure and settled. When the conferees moved on to Geneva, Hymans successfully proposed a League Conference to organise a tariff truce. With others, he confidently predicted: *We would see better times open before us.*[9]

11

The Pre-war Decade

1930 was Belgium's centennial year. The celebrations took place under darkening skies, economically and politically, the latter both internally and internationally. Within Belgium, the Flemish majority (over 60 per cent) was more hostile to France and impatient for faster cultural equality. On paper it had achieved much, but application of the laws was spotty. Economically, the New York Stock Exchange crash in October 1929 led to a period of uncertainty, impacting export-dependent states like Belgium and causing recession in some, including Germany, before the world slid into an economic depression of unprecedented scale in 1931. Meanwhile, on 30 June 1930 the last Allied troops left the Rhineland, releasing a nationalist explosion of such dimensions that Adolf Hitler's National Socialist (Nazi) Party came from nowhere in Germany's September 1930 elections to become the second largest party of 26. As a consequence, the optimism of 1929 was gone and observers in Geneva remarked, 'Europe in the autumn of 1930 was filled with talk of the dangers of war' and 'fear and anxiety were real and widespread'.[1]

Paul Hymans remained Foreign Minister without

interruption from 1927 to 1934 and, after a brief hiatus, on into 1935, in part because no party commanded a Parliamentary majority but either of the larger parties could do so in coalition with the Liberals. Until 1935, his generation governed Belgium. As Flemish resentment grew into talk of federalism or separatism, the economy worsened with strikes and mounting unemployment, a generational gap added to other divisions and the international scene became more alarming, especially after Hitler became the Weimar Republic's last Chancellor on 30 January 1933. Ministries became shorter as political turbulence increased. Under these circumstances, Belgium's foreign policy became more modest.

Already in the late 1920s Belgium had favoured concessions to maintain Stresemann (who died in October 1929) in office and prevent right-wing ascendancy in Germany. It wanted to end the occupation of the Rhineland and to avoid being dominated by France, which rarely consulted before acting. In November 1930, it decided that 'Belgium will take up arms only if respecting its international engagements and the pressing demands of its independence and territorial integrity so command'.[2] This was to be a policy of full independence wherein action would be in concert with Britain, whose support the whole country desired. On 4 March 1931, Hymans provided a fuller statement, approved by Cabinet and King, in which he argued that the 1920 military accord with France was not an alliance but strictly a technical agreement in the context of the First World War's aftermath but now overlapped and complemented by Locarno, as France agreed. *Our policy remains one of peace ... It is inspired by the generous and clairvoyant ideal of European cooperation and agreement whose progressive and slow realisation M. Briand seeks with admirable understanding of the*

practical necessities and moral laws of our times.[3] The bases
of Belgian policy were understood to be the League, Locarno
and the Kellogg-Briand Pact. Until Hymans left the Cabinet
altogether in 1936, this exposition remained the official statement of Belgian foreign policy.

Though Hymans tried to narrow the military accord, he
opposed renunciation as unduly offensive to France, which
alone could provide rapid rescue. He favoured an independent
policy, not neutrality or isolationism. Now a fully seasoned
diplomat, he was, especially after 1930, more realistic about
the European situation and Belgium's role in it. He was also
tired. After a brief illness, he considered resignation, saying
in February 1931 in English, *I am fed up.*[4] He stayed, however,
and his role at Geneva ensured his continuing prominence
despite his country's more modest policy.

Most especially, the Japanese conquest of Manchuria,
starting in September 1931, led the League Council to dis-
patch a slow-moving investigative commission under Lord
Lytton of Britain and then to call a special Assembly session
to address the problem. Both bodies were hamstrung by a
unanimity requirement for decisions but, thanks to a ruling
by Hymans as President of the first Assembly, its resolu-
tions required only a majority. When it met in March 1932,
Hymans was overwhelmingly elected President. He directed
a special committee which achieved a definitive end to hostilities at Shanghai, rejected Japan's claim that China was
not really a state, sought Japanese withdrawal and rallied
opinion. Otherwise, it could only await the Lytton Report.
When it arrived, the committee and then the Assembly on 24
February 1933 endorsed most of its recommendations supporting China. Japan walked out and left the League a month
later, the first major Power to do so.

By then, Hitler was Chancellor of Germany, and the League Disarmament Conference in Geneva, which opened in February 1932 and lasted into 1934, was struggling to cope with that fact. Hymans led the Belgian delegation and was elected Vice-President of the Conference, which Belgium strongly supported. Hymans himself was not optimistic, foreseeing failure and saying: *We must hope, but we must anticipate everything.*[6] He did not think small states should lead the way and opposed further Belgian disarmament, especially unilaterally. But any limitation on Great Power armaments

> **The little states can help the Great Powers, but it is never little states which put the universe in danger.**
> **PAUL HYMANS**[5]

would be a blessing. France sought security and Germany equality, but if Germany gained equality France, smaller and weaker, had no security, so the Conference did not progress. Hymans favoured interim partial steps, giving Hitler a few apparent satisfactions and setting controls on future expansion. He deplored French rigidity, born of fear of Hitler and of the 'lean years' when low birthrates during 1915–18 would shrink its army. He sought greater French flexibility, especially after Germany left the Conference and the League in October 1933, and convinced Foreign Minister Louis Barthou but not the French Cabinet. Thereafter Anglo-French disagreement was acute and Hymans sought to address it, inviting Barthou and Eden to lunch at Geneva. Barthou said, 'It's quite simple. Belgium has a wife, France, and a mistress, England. That is why Belgium pays more attention to the mistress than the wife.' Hymans riposted: *Why not say that I have two mistresses?*[7] But no drollery could improve the Anglo-French relationship or salvage the Disarmament Conference, which faded away.

Meanwhile, another Conference had been held in Lausanne in June and July 1932 to arrange a concealed end to German reparations. During it, Hymans signed with Dutch and Luxembourgeois diplomats the Convention of Ouchy (an adjacent village) reducing tariff barriers among the three states. Further measures of economic cooperation followed in later years. Earlier, in December 1930, all three states had joined with the Scandinavian nations in the Oslo Convention also against tariff barriers and for closer economic cooperation. The 'Oslo Group' quickly developed, meeting in Geneva and elsewhere to seek, but not always find, a common policy on European issues. Gradually, Belgian-Dutch relations improved. These innovations of the 1930s contained the seeds of the Benelux customs union negotiated during the Second World War in London by governments in exile and contributed in part to the later development of the Common Market and the European Union.

In the 1930s as the Depression deepened, economic issues dominated most policy. During his last brief stint at the Foreign Ministry in 1934–5, Hymans focused on commercial agreements, which he had not neglected earlier, while Theunis as Prime Minister struggled with monetary crisis. In 1928 Hymans had laboriously negotiated a commercial treaty with France approved by the Belgian Parliament. This brought real benefits for several years until France introduced a quota system which effectively destroyed the Treaty. Hymans gained some alleviations, but economic disputes with France continued in an era of growing global economic nationalism. He represented Belgium at the abortive 1933 London World Economic Conference, where he became Vice-President by acclamation, and tried without success for tariff reduction at Geneva, falling back on regional arrangements such as Ouchy and Oslo, and individual agreements, which he succeeded in negotiating with several nations, including the United States. Hitler's accession to power brought subversion and occasional incidents in Eupen-Malmédy along with signs that Germany had not renounced the two Cantons (which it annexed in May 1940) and also a threat to halt monthly payments on the 1929 mark agreement. With difficulty Hymans managed to extend them another year.

Despite Hymans' efforts, by 1934–5 Belgium's economic condition was parlous and was aggravating all divisions, whether linguistic, class, political, generational or economic. Belgium seemed to be fragmenting, but the entire nation came to an abrupt halt in February 1934 upon the death of King Albert while rock-climbing. His heir, Leopold III (1934–51), was intelligent and conscientious but young and inexperienced – and shattered in 1935 by Queen Astrid's death in an automobile accident. He was quickly embroiled in yet another divisive controversy, one on which Belgium's survival depended in more than one sense.

Hymans supported the Disarmament Conference as long as there was a chance of success, but thereafter Germany's increasingly overt rearmament demanded a response to lengthen military service from eight to 18 months and to modernise Belgium's defences. The Defence Minister (who headed the military establishment in peacetime) from 1932 to 1936 was Albert Devèze, a francophile Walloon who favoured a frontier defence on the Albert Canal (completed in 1939), Liège and the Meuse. The King, Albert and then Leopold, who was military commander in wartime, together with royal military advisers and successive Chiefs of the General Staff, preferred a fighting retreat to Ghent, Antwerp and the line of the Scheldt as enabling a prolonged defence, British relief efforts and keeping the army intact. But their plan implied early abandonment of the Belgian Walloon province of Luxembourg. It also failed to meet France's defence requirements.

Through the inter-war era, France's defence strategy rested on fighting the next war in Belgium on the line of the Meuse, assuming early entry of the French army. Construction from 1929 of the Maginot Line, that string of massive, half-sunken forts along the Franco-German frontier, altered nothing since extension of the Line on the Belgian border was not feasible. Flemish fear of vassalage to French policy was great, but the situation was tolerable while danger was remote. Now it was real, and Flemish parliamentary leaders, supported by some Socialists hostile to rearmament, would not accept any military reform bill until the 1920 accord was abrogated. Moreover, Marshal Henri-Philippe Pétain, French hero of the First World War, said if war came, the French army would enter Belgium whether invited or not. Inquiries in Paris did not elicit satisfactory answers.

In French eyes, the 1920 accord remained entirely in force and constituted an alliance, though it had been almost a dead letter for 15 years. To Belgian leaders, it was a limited technical agreement which had been overtaken by events and supplanted by Locarno. An exchange of letters in 1931 subordinated it to the League and Locarno, but there remained clauses for the defence of Luxembourg without its consent, for French defence of the Belgian coast, and for immediate military mobilisation if Germany mobilised. Belgium much feared that France would demand Belgian mobilisation and passage for French troops (and perhaps more) if Germany mobilised against Poland.

Hymans tried repeatedly to narrow the accord, gaining no more than the 1931 letters. Knowing only a parallel agreement

with Britain would render it acceptable to the Flemish majority, he tried for that in 1934. Though he failed, the Foreign
Secretary told the House of Commons in July that the territorial integrity of Belgium was no less important to Britain
than in the past, and Prime Minister Stanley Baldwin declared
in the name of the Cabinet that in an aviation age Britain's
defensive frontier was not at Dover but at the Rhine. While
welcome, these statements did not suffice in Belgium's political context. Hymans advised the young King: *If she* [Belgium]
*follows France, she may, step by step, find herself in a war
against Germany with France and its central European allies
without the support of England. She would risk material
destruction and the tearing asunder of her national unity.... .
The risk of a political war, at the side of France alone, would
be rejected by a large part of the country.*[8] The 1935 Franco-
Soviet Treaty, which horrified most Belgians, worsened the
domestic political problem just when France sought closer
military staff arrangements.

The internal and external controversy over Belgium's
defence was approaching a climax as Belgium neared bank-
ruptcy, and devaluation of the currency was imperative while
both strikes and unrest mounted. After first de Broqueville
and then Theunis failed to solve the economic emergency, it
was time for new men. In March 1935, Paul van Zeeland,
a young non-political financier, became Prime Minister and
Foreign Minister in a Cabinet of markedly younger men. A
senior leader of each party, including Hymans, remained as
Minister without Portfolio. The new leaders coped well with
the economic crisis but found other matters, including military reform, more difficult.

The worsening international situation, especially as Hitler
announced conscription and a new air force, made Belgian

efforts to edge away from France without a British counter-balance more difficult and sometimes affected the economy as well. In the crisis created by Italy's invasion of Abyssinia (Ethiopia), which became acute in late 1935, Belgium voted at the League for economic sanctions and dutifully applied them. It did so unhappily in view of religious and dynastic ties, damage to the economy as Italy was a good customer, and potential damage to security since Italy was a Locarno Guarantor which Belgium did not want to see driven into Hitler's camp. By the time sanctions ended in the summer of 1936, Hymans knew the League was in crisis and said so openly. By then, the Spanish Civil War had become an inter-national issue as well. Belgium followed Britain and France into non-intervention both because the two Powers actually agreed and because the Spanish question only further divided a divided nation, and no other policy was possible.

As the international situation deteriorated, so did Bel-gium's domestic politics, and the military bill suffered pre-liminary defeats. The Catholic party seemed to be breaking into linguistic halves, and authoritarian fascist movements, some of the Flemish ones openly separatist, were burgeon-ing. Most notable were the Flemish National Front and Leon Degrelle's Rexist Movement (from *Christus Rex* – Christ the King – the name of a Catholic publishing house). Flemish hostility to the French accord, which several members of the 1920 Cabinet swore they had never seen or approved, was total. In desperation, van Zeeland told France the military accord had to end for domestic political reasons. Thus, an exchange of letters on 6 March 1936,[9] published at once, abrogated it but too late to quiet opposition, especially since staff talks under the Locarno Pact remained.

The next day, Hitler remilitarised the Rhineland, bringing

his army to the Franco-Belgian borders and effectively destroying the Locarno Pact. The other Locarno Powers met in London, producing a provisional Anglo-French-Belgian mutual guarantee until some 'new Locarno' could replace it and an agreement on three-way staff talks.[10] The former gave Belgium a new obligation, to defend Britain, and the latter, which Britain ensured were minimal, revealed that Britain could provide only two divisions within 20 or 30 days of a war's outbreak. In short, Britain could not serve as a counterbalance to Germany. Meanwhile, Hitler launched a flurry of proposals designed to spin negotiations out interminably and prevent reprisals or a new Locarno, which never materialised.

In an acutely disturbed atmosphere, domestic and foreign, in May Belgium held an election, which Hymans termed his last. He was easily returned, but in general extremism triumphed. The Communists tripled their seats, the Flemish National Front doubled theirs, and the Rexists, newly a party, took ten per cent of the vote and 21 seats. The Catholic Party was much weakened, the Socialists now the largest despite sizeable losses. The Liberals lost fewer seats but much influence because no party could now command a majority in combination with them. A three-party Cabinet resulted, again under van Zeeland. Hymans endorsed the choice of Paul-Henri Spaak as Foreign Minister and himself declined a portfolio but remained on the Diplomatic Committee.

The election solved nothing, nor did a general strike. In July Spaak declared that he wanted 'a foreign policy which is exclusively and wholly Belgian'.[11] While the implications were unclear, he and his staff wished to end Belgium's guarantee of Great Powers. In an ominous situation, that burden was too heavy for a tiny state. As the Rexists and the Flemish National Union joined in alliance, which briefly appeared very threatening, and the military bill remained stalled, King Leopold on 14 October addressed the Cabinet in blunt language not meant for publication, urging a completely independent policy of no alliances or foreign commitments in order to avoid war.[12] The Cabinet unanimously adopted the King's statement and, at Vandervelde's suggestion, published it at once without diplomatic preparation and apparently without thought to foreign reaction, which was sharp. Belgians saw little new in the speech, but queries from Paris confirmed that Belgium wished to guarantee nobody in a new Locarno. When van Zeeland said so openly in December, the military bill, now a compromise plan with 17 months service acceptable to France, was enacted at once.

In a speech in January 1937, Hitler offered to guarantee Belgium as a neutral and did so in October. In April Britain and France released Belgium from its obligations under Locarno and the 19 March 1936 London Accord. They reiterated their own commitments to defend Belgium subject only to its own self-defence if invaded.[13] At long last, thanks essentially to Hitler, Belgium gained the free hand and Allied guarantees which Hymans had spent 15 years seeking. He was meticulous about not commenting on foreign policy when he no longer ran it and he understood that burdens Belgium had assumed in a time of no danger were too great as war threatened. He endorsed an independent policy in the Chamber but privately was disturbed by growing neutralism and isolationism, which he knew were unlikely to save Belgium. He favoured a free hand but fidelity to traditional friends.

Upon his retirement from the Cabinet in June 1936, Hymans remained the Liberal leader and head of the Party's Parliamentary faction. He read voraciously, wrote a good deal including his diplomatic memoirs, and resumed his early activity as a historian, participating in a parliamentary history of Belgium and sketching out the third and final volume of his biography of Frère-Orban. Especially, he became President of his beloved University of Brussels, presiding at meetings of the administrative council of which he had been a member since 1907 and introducing more courses in Flemish in the law faculty. And, between streams of visitors, he gloomily watched the approach of war.

When Hitler invaded Belgium in May 1940, Hymans, now Dean of the Ministers of State, arranged that he and two others remain attached to the Cabinet should it have to leave Brussels. This time, removal to Ostend and Sainte-Adresse came with terrifying speed, followed by further removals southward. With the shock of the King's surrender and the Cabinet's decision to remain an Allied belligerent, he remained with the government, counseling close adherence to the constitution and moderation in word and deed. Only when the French armistice ended any possibility of political action by the Belgian Cabinet on French soil did he take leave of the government.

Hymans considered returning to Brussels to his duties at the university but discovered he had already been replaced there and that all advice was against return. Accordingly he and his wife settled in modest quarters in a seaside hotel in Nice. Here he had ample time to write, but all his files were in Brussels. At age 75, gradually his health declined and on 6 March 1941* he died of a heart attack, having said earlier

---

*A number of sources, including several Internet ones, report the date of Hymans' death as 8 March. However, the extremely carefully edited posthumous Hymans *Mémoires* (2, p 984) lists the date as 6 March. Furthermore, the New York Times of 8 March 1941 carried an obituary saying Hymans had died on 6 March. Given the extreme unlikelihood of

on: *Thanks to God, my life has been a happy one.*[14]

Paul Hymans was indeed happy to spend his life serving Belgium. He and it learned together about the world of Great Power diplomacy, haltingly at first, discovering the hard way that effective diplomacy rests on power, which his beloved Belgium lacked. As Foreign Minister, he made mistakes early on both from inexperience and, at the Paris Peace Conference, from caring too much, trying too hard and trusting the faithful Guarantors too consistently, though how much difference his missteps made is arguable. In any event, the decisions made at Paris by the Great Powers dictated Belgium's role and course through most of the inter-war era, providing a legacy and framework of prominence, powerlessness, insecurity and minimal diplomatic weight.

In some of its characteristics, Belgium was a fairly typical small state, perpetually seeking a voice, searching for security and active at the League of Nations, usually in the person of Hymans. In other respects, its role in the war and in the post-war years was distinctive, leading to startling diplomatic prominence. Belgium was neither a new state nor a devotee of the 'new diplomacy'. Though nearly 90 years old in 1919, its past history meant that in some ways it was more adolescent than adult, still needing support and protection. Nonetheless, while it upheld the League, it did not rely on it. Nor was it a convert to the old diplomacy, in which it had scarcely participated. Hymans and his successors dealt with the post-war Europe they found after the Peace Conference, quickly shedding illusions and learning the ways of the Great Powers.

---

a (misdated) report of an 8 March 1941 death in Nice being reported in wartime in the morning edition of a New York paper on the same day, that appears conclusive.

None of the Kingdom's leaders could bring themselves to accept that for Belgium security and independence were incompatible in view of the clashing policies of their three Great Power neighbours. Hymans sought to balance between and rest upon Britain and France, as did other Belgian Foreign Ministers of the era. Although this policy was probably the only possible one in Belgium's internal and external circumstances, it foundered on British indifference and determination not to have to defend Belgium again along with French arrogance and self-preoccupied fear of Germany, as well as Germany's truculent revisionism and Belgium's inability to provide security for itself. Ultimately, Hitler's increasingly blatant aggressive nationalism forced reappraisal in both Britain and Belgium.

The efforts of Hymans were dogged, extended and steadily more skilful over time. Nonetheless, between the Wars it was beyond the capacity of Hymans or any other Foreign Minister to solve Belgium's fundamental dilemma of its exposed geographic position and lack of power. Paul Hymans, who became a diplomat in Belgium's first nightmarish wartime experience, died – again in exile – during its second and did not live to see it finally find the security he had so determinedly sought in a new and larger post-war constellation of Western Powers created in response to the Cold War.

Notes

1 The Crossroads of Europe

1. Daniel H Thomas, *The Guarantee of Belgian Independence and Neutrality in European Diplomacy, 1830s–1930s* (D H Thomas Publishing Co, Kingston, Rhode Island: 1983) pp 13–14.

2. Great Britain, Foreign Office, British and Foreign State Papers (Her Majesty's Stationery Office, London: 1856) 27, pp 1001, 994.

3. David Stevenson, 'Battlefield or Barrier? Rearmament and Military Planning in Belgium, 1902–1914', *The International History Review*, 24 (2007) p 475.

4. Stevenson, 'Battlefield or Barrier?', pp 493–4.

2 The First Career

1. Robert Fenaux, *Paul Hymans, un homme, un temps* (Office de publicité, Brussels: 1946) p 53.

2. Fenaux, *Paul Hymans*, p 401.

3. Fenaux, *Paul Hymans*, p 402.

3 In the Crucible

1. Commandant Adrien Gerlache de Gomery, *Belgium in Wartime*, tr Bernard Miall (George H Doran, New York: 1916) p 25.
2. The most accessible source on these points is Larry Zuckerman, *The Rape of Belgium* (New York University Press, New York: 2004) pp 86–7, 169–70, 204.
3. Bernard A Cook, *Belgium: A History* (Peter Lang, New York: 2004) pp 99–100.
4. Jean Massart, *The Secret Press in Belgium* (E P Dutton, New York: 1918) p 12.
5. Paul Hymans, *Mémoires*, Volume 2 (Éditions de l'Institute Solvay, Brussels: 1958) pp 914–15, hereafter Hymans 2.
6. Great Britain, Admiralty, Naval Intelligence Division, Geographic Handbook Series, *A Manual of Belgium and the Adjoining Territories* (His Majesty's Stationery Office, London: n d) p 200.
7. Hymans, *Mémoires*, Volume 1 (Éditions de l'Institute Solvay, Brussels: 1958) p 181, hereafter Hymans 1.

4 Baptism by Total Immersion

1. Hymans 1, p 335.
2. Stephen Bonsal, *Unfinished Business* (Doubleday Doran, Garden City, New York: 1944) pp 59, 162.
3. Pierre van Zuylen, *Les Mains Libres* (L'Éditions universelle, Brussels: 1950) p 100.
4. Hymans 1, p 337.
5. Zuckerman, *The Rape of Belgium*, p 221.
6. Jonathan E Helmreich, *Belgium and Europe: A Study in Small Power Diplomacy* (Mouton, The Hague: 1976) p 202.

7. Bonsal, *Unfinished Business*, p 162.

8. David Hunter Miller, *My Diary at the Conference of Paris with Documents*, 21 Volumes (privately printed, n p: n d) 5, p 101, hereafter Hunter Miller, *Diary*, 5.

9. *Papers Relating to the Foreign Relations of the United States: The Paris Peace Conference, 1919* (Government Printing Office, Washington: 1942–7) 3, pp 959, 969.

10. Sally Marks, *Innocent Abroad: Belgium at the Paris Peace Conference of 1919* (University of North Carolina Press, Chapel Hill: 1981) p 112.

11. Paul Mantoux, *Les Déliberations du conseil des quatres (24 mars–28 juin 1919)*, 2 Volumes (Editions du Centre National de la Recherche Scientifique, Paris) 1, pp 92–5.

12. Hymans 1, p 450.

13. Fenaux, *Paul Hymans*, p 237.

5 Territorial Aspirations

1. E H Kossman, *The Low Countries, 1780–1940* (Clarendon Press, Oxford: 1978) p 581.

2. Netherlands, *Documenten betreffende de buitenslandse politiek van Nederland, 1919–1942: Periode A, 1919–1930*, 8 Volumes to date (Martinus Nijhoff, The Hague: 1976–), Rijks Geschiedkundige Publicatiën, Grote Serie 156, p 125, hereafter *DuD*, R G P 156.

3. Fenaux, *Paul Hymans,* p 135.

4. Margaret Macmillan, *Paris, 1919* (Random House, New York: 2002) p 278.

5. Alan Sharp, 'Holding Up the Flag of Britain ...', in M Dockrill and J Fisher, *The Paris Peace Conference, 1919: Peace without Victory?* (Palgrave, Basingstoke: 2001) p 38.

6. Bernard Auffray, *Pierre de Margerie (1861–1942) et la vie diplomatique de son temps* (C Klincksieck, Paris: 1976) p 375.

7. Marks, *Innocent Abroad*, p 249.

8. Hymans 1, pp 339–43.

9. Hymans 1, p 343.

10. United States, Department of State, *Papers Relating to the Foreign Relations of the United States: The Paris Peace Conference, 1919*, 13 Volumes (Government Printing Office, Washington: 1942–7) 5, p 420, hereafter *FRUS PPC*, 5

11. *FRUS PPC*, 5, p 459.

12. Wm Roger Louis, *Ruanda-Urundi, 1884–1919* (Clarendon Press, Oxford: 1963) p 241.

6 Economic Issues

1. Marks, *Innocent Abroad*, p 177.

2. Marks, *Innocent Abroad*, p 182.

3. Great Britain, House of Lords, Record Office, Balfour to Lloyd George, 3 April 1919, Lloyd George Papers F/3/h/20.

4. Inga Floto, *Colonel House in Paris* (Princeton University Press, Princeton, New Jersey: 1980) p 192.

5. Hymans 1, p 407.

6. *De Standaard* (Brussels), 3 May 1919, p 1.

7. *FRUS PPC*, 5, p 447.

8. Rolande Depoortere, *La Question des reparations allemandes dans la politique étrangère de la Belgique après la première guerre mondiale, 1919–1925* (Académie royale de Belgique, Brussels: 1997) p 39.

9. Marks, *Innocent Abroad*, p 204.

10. *The New York Times,* 20 June 1919, p 2.

7 Treaty Revision?

1. André Tardieu, *The Truth about the Treaty* (Bobbs-Merrill: Indianapolis, 1921) p 220.
2. Hunter Miller, *Diary*, 4, p 494.
3. *DuD*, R G P 156, p 674.
4. Fenaux, *Paul Hymans*, p 203.
5. Netherlands, *Bescheiden betreffende de buitenlandse politiek van Nederland, 1848–1919: Derde Periode, 1899–1919,* 8 Volumes in 10 (Martinus Nijhoff, The Hague: 1957–74) Rijks Geschiedkundige Publicatien, Grote Serie 117, pp 1063–4, hereafter *DuD*, R G P 117.
6. *DuD*, R G P 117, pp 172–3.
7. Marks, *Innocent Abroad*, p 269.
8. Belgium, Ministry of Foreign Affairs, Hymans memo, 7 June 1919, file Indépendance, neutralité 1919/1.
9. Great Britain, Foreign Office, *Documents on British Foreign Policy, 1919–1939*, First Series, 27 Volumes (Her Majesty's Stationery Office, London: 1947–82), 5, pp 517–19, hereafter *DBFP*, 1st Ser, 5.
10. *DBFP*, 1st Ser, 5, p 852.
11. *DuD*, R G P 156, p 676.
12. van Zuylen, *Les Mains libres*, p 98.
13. Hymans 2, p 491.
14. Fenaux, *Paul Hymans*, p 239.

8 The Search for Security

1. Hymans 2, p 551.
2. Fernand van Langenhove, *La Belgique en quête de sécurité, 1920–1940* (La Renaissance du livre, Brussels: 1969) p 17.
3. Tardieu, *The Truth about the Treaty*, p 217.
4. Tardieu, *The Truth about the Treaty*, p 217.

5. Éric Bussière, *La France, la Belgique, et l'organisation économique de l'Europe* (Comité pour l'histoire économique et financière de la France, Paris: 1992) p 42.

6. Marks, *Innocent Abroad*, p 249.

7. Gilbert Trausch, 'Les Relations franco-belges à propos de la question luxembourgeois (1914–1922)', in Actes du colloque de Metz, *Les Relations franco-belges de 1830 à 1934* (Centre de recherches relations internationals, Université de Metz, Metz: 1975) p 291.

8. Van Langenhove, *La Belgique en quête de sécurité*, p 30.

9. Marks, *Innocent Abroad*, p 345.

10. van Zuylen, *Les Mains libres*, p 117.

11. For text, see Belgium, Académie royale de Belgique, *Documents diplomatiques belges, 1920–1940*, Ch de Visscher and F Van Langenhove (eds), 5 Volumes (Palais des academies, Brussels: 1964–6) 1, pp 405–8, hereafter *DDB*.

12. Helmreich, *Belgium and Europe*, p 236 and footnote 22, pp 307–8.

13. van Zuylen, *Les Mains libres*, p 119.

14. Helmreich, *Belgium and Europe*, p 230.

15. Great Britain, Parliament, Cmd. 2525, *Final Protocol of the Locarno Conference, 1925* (His Majesty's Stationery Office, London: 1925).

16. Belgium, parliament, Chambre des Représentants, *Compte rendu, 1918-19* (Brussels: 1919) p 904.

9 The Hinge of the Entente

1. Fenaux, *Paul Hymans*, pp 131–2.

2. Helmreich, *Belgium and Europe*, p 226.

3. Weimar Republic, Akten der Reichskanzlei, *Das Kabinett Cuno*, ed Karl-Heinz Harbeck (Harald Boldt Verlag, Boppard am Rhein: 1968) p 192.
4. Helmreich, *Belgium and Europe*, pp 261–2.
5. George A Riddell, *Lord Riddell's Intimate Diary of the Peace Conference and After, 1918–1923* (Reynal & Hitchcock, New York: 1934) p 210.
6. Riddell, *Lord Riddell's Intimate Diary*, p 68.
7. Helmreich, *Belgium and Europe*, p 304.
8. Fenaux, *Paul Hymans*, p 298.
9. Jacques Bariéty, *Les Relations franco-allemandes après la première guerre mondiale* (Editions Pédone, Paris: 1977) p 373.
10. Stephen A Schuker, *The End of French Predominance in Europe* (University of North Carolina Press, Chapel Hill: 1976) p 245.
11. Fenaux, *Paul Hymans*, p 302.
12. Schuker, *End of French Predominance*, p 189.
13. Schuker, *End of French Predominance*, p 314.
14. Manfred J Enssle, *Stresemann's Territorial Revisionism* (Franz Steiner Verlag, Wiesbaden: 1980) p 70.
15. Bariéty, *Les Relations franco-allemandes*, p 660.
16. Van Langenhove, *La Belgique en quête de sécurité*, p 51.
17. Enssle, *Stresemann's Territorial Revisionism*, p 112.
18. *DDB*, 2, pp 345–6.
19. Zara Steiner, *The Lights that Failed* (Oxford University Press, Oxford: 2005) p 420.
20. *DDB*, 2 p 532.
21. For text, see *DDB*, 2, p 532.

10 The Post-War Decade

1. Anthony Eden, Earl of Avon, *The Memoirs of Anthony Eden: Facing the Dictators* (Houghton Mifflin, Boston: 1962) p 104.
2. Enssle, *Stresemann's Territorial Revisionism*, p 90.
3. Fenaux, *Paul Hymans*, p 266.
4. Fenaux, *Paul Hymans*, p 257.
5. van Zuylen, *Les Mains libres*, p 222.
6. Elmer Bendiner, *A Time for Angels: The Tragicomic History of the League of Nations* (Alfred A Knopf, New York: 1975) p 230.
7. Hymans 2, p 926.
8. Hymans 2, p 928.
9. Hymans 2, p 929.

11 The Pre-War Decade

1. F P Walters, *A History of the League of Nations*, 1 Volume ed (Oxford University Press, Oxford: 1960) p 439.
2. *DDB*, 2, p 622.
3. David O Kieft, *Belgium's Return to Neutrality* (Clarendon Press, Oxford: 1972) p 3.
4. Hymans 2, p 625.
5. Hymans 2, pp 931–2.
6. Fenaux, *Paul Hymans*, p 288.
7. Bendiner, *A Time for Angels*, p 301.
8. *DDB*, 3, p 361.
9. For text see *DDB*, 3, pp 494–5.
10. For text see *DBFP*, Second Series, 21 Volumes (Her Majesty's Stationery Office, London: 1946–84) 16, pp 192–7.
11. Kieft, *Belgium's Return to Neutrality*, p 110.

12. For text see *DDB*, 4, pp 323–9.
13. For text see *DDB*, 4, pp 564–5. English text in *The Times* (London), 26 April 1937, p 14.
14. Fenaux, *Paul Hymans,* p 400.

Chronology

YEAR	AGE	THE LIFE AND THE LAND
1839		19 Apr: Treaties of London between Belgium and Holland and with the Great Powers.
1865		23 Mar: Paul Hymans born at Ixelles. 17 Dec: Accession of Leopold II.
1867	2	11 May: Treaty of London guarantees neutrality of Luxembourg.
1870	5	9 Aug: Prussia guarantees Belgian neutrality. 11 Aug: Britain and France guarantee Belgian neutrality.
1884	19	May: Hymans becomes assistant librarian, Chamber of Representatives.
1885	20	Hymans awarded doctor of laws degree, Free University of Brussels; joins Brussels bar. Congo established as personal possession of Leopold II.
1897	32	Hymans begins to teach at Free University of Brussels.
1898	33	14 Apr Hymans marries Mlle Thérèse Goldschmidt.

YEAR	HISTORY	CULTURE
1839	First Opium War between Britain and China begins.	Edgar Allen Poe, *The Fall of the House of Usher*.
1865	US Civil War ends: Confederates surrender at Appomattox.	Lewis Carroll, *Alice's Adventures in Wonderland*.
1867	North German Confederation founded. South African diamond fields discovered.	Anthony Trollope, *The Last Chronicle of Barset*.
1870	Franco-Prussian War: Napoleon III defeated at Sedan, Third Republic proclaimed, Paris besieged.	Jules Verne, *Twenty Thousand Leagues Under the Sea*. Richard Wagner, *Die Walküre*.
1884	Berlin Conference of 14 nations on African affairs. Gold discovered in the Transvaal.	Mark Twain, *Huckleberry Finn*.
1885	General Gordon killed in fall of Khartoum to the Mahdi. Germany annexes Tanganyika and Zanzibar.	Guy de Maupassant, *Bel Ami*. H Rider Haggard, *King Solomon's Mines*. W S Gilbert and Arthur Sullivan, *The Mikado*.
1897	Britain's Queen Victoria celebrates Diamond Jubilee.	H G Wells, *The Invisible Man*.
1898	General Kitchener defeats Mahdists at Omdurman. Germany's Otto von Bismarck dies.	Oscar Wilde, *The Ballad of Reading Gaol*.

YEAR	AGE	THE LIFE AND THE LAND
1900	35	27 May: Hymans elected to Chamber from Brussels.
1903	38	Hymans elected President of Liberal League.
1906	41	Hymans becomes professor at Free University of Brussels.
1907	42	9 Nov: Hymans becomes permanent member of Council of Administration, Free University of Brussels.
1908	43	20 Aug: Leopold II cedes Congo to Belgium.
1909	44	14 Dec: Leopold II signs Military Reform Bill. 23 Dec: Albert I enthroned.

YEAR	HISTORY	CULTURE
1900	Second Boer War: Mafeking relieved, Johannesburg and Pretoria captured.	Sigmund Freud, *The Interpretation of Dreams*.
1903	Beginning of Entente Cordiale: King Edward VII of Britain visits Paris, French President Loubet visits London.	Film: *The Great Train Robbery*.
1906	King Edward VII of Britain and Kaiser Wilhelm II of Germany meet.	John Galsworthy, *A Man of Property*.
1907	Peace Conference held at The Hague.	Joseph Conrad, *The Secret Agent*.
1908	*The Daily Telegraph* publishes German Kaiser Wilhelm II's hostile remarks towards England.	Kenneth Grahame, *The Wind in the Willows*.
1909	Britain's King Edward VII makes state visits to Berlin and Rome.	H G Wells, *Tono-Bungay*.

YEAR	AGE	THE LIFE AND THE LAND
1914	49	2 Aug: Germany occupies Luxembourg; German ultimatum to Belgium; Hymans becomes Minister of State.
		3 Aug: Belgium rejects ultimatum.
		4 Aug: Germany invades and declares war on Belgium.
		5 Aug: Anglo-French-Russian Declaration of London.
		16 Aug: Last Liège forts fall.
		18 Aug: Belgian government to Antwerp.
		20 Aug: Brussels falls.
		22 Aug: German attack on Congo.
		25–30 Aug: Sack of Louvain.
		28 Aug: Austria-Hungary declares war on Belgium.
		30 Aug–9 Oct: Belgian mission (including Hymans) to US.
		10 Oct: Antwerp falls.
		13 Oct: Belgian government moves to France.
		18–30 Oct: Battle of the Yser.
		22 Oct–22 Nov: First Battle of Ypres.
1915	50	28 Feb: Hymans appointed Belgian minister to London.
1916	51	18 Jan: Hymans enters Cabinet without portfolio.
		Feb: Formal Belgian Cabinet decision against compulsory neutrality.
		14 Feb: Declaration of Sainte-Adresse pledges Belgium's post-war independence, participation in peace negotiations and indemnification of damages
		Apr–May: Belgian forces overrun Ruanda, Urundi.
		13 Sep: Belgium rejects British military agreement.
		19 Sep: Belgian forces take Tabora.

YEAR	HISTORY	CULTURE
1914	Archduke Franz Ferdinand of Austria-Hungary and wife assassinated in Sarajevo. First World War begins: Russians defeated in Battles of Tannenberg and Masurian Lakes.	James Joyce, *Dubliners*. Theodore Dreiser, *The Titan*. Gustav Holst, *The Planets*. Matisse, *The Red Studio*. Georges Braque, *Music*. Film: Charlie Chaplin in *Making a Living*.
1915	First World War: Battles of Neuve Chapelle and Loos, 'Shells Scandal', Gallipoli campaign.	John Buchan, *The Thirty-Nine Steps*. Film: *The Birth of a Nation*.
1916	First World War: Battles of Verdun, the Somme and Jutland. US President Woodrow Wilson re-elected. Wilson issues Peace Note to belligerents in European war. David Lloyd George becomes British Prime Minister. Development and use of first effective tanks.	Lionel Curtis, *The Commonwealth of Nations*. James Joyce, *Portrait of an Artist as a Young Man*. Film: *Intolerance*.

YEAR	AGE	THE LIFE AND THE LAND
1917	52	10 Jan: Belgium states war aims to President Wilson.
		Feb: Belgium evacuates Tabora and part of German East Africa.
		9 Jun: Ribot Declaration on Luxembourg.
		20 Oct: Hymans leaves London.
		22 Oct: Hymans becomes Minister of Economic Affairs.
		24 Dec: Belgium states war aims to Pope Benedict XV.
1918	53	1 Jan: Hymans becomes Foreign Minister.
		8 Jan: Wilson's Fourteen Points state Belgium must be evacuated and restored.
		Sep: Liberation of Belgium begins.
		21 Nov: Delacroix Cabinet installed; US Third Army arrives in Luxembourg.
		22 Nov: Foch arrives in Luxembourg City; Albert address to Parliament in Brussels promises reforms.

YEAR	HISTORY	CULTURE
1917	First World War: Battle of Passchendaele (Third Ypres); British and Commonwealth forces take Jerusalem; USA declares war on Germany. February Revolution in Russia. German and Russian delegates sign armistice at Brest-Litovsk.	P G Wodehouse, *The Man With Two Left Feet.* T S Eliot, *Prufrock and Other Observations.* Leon Feuchtwanger, *Jud Suess.* Film: *Easy Street.*
1918	First World War: Peace Treaty of Brest-Litovsk signed between Russia and Central Powers; German Spring offensives on Western Front fail; Allied offensives on Western Front have German army in full retreat; Armistice signed between Allies and Germany; German Fleet surrenders. Kaiser Wilhelm II of Germany abdicates.	Alexander Blok, *The Twelve.* Gerald Manley Hopkins, *Poems.* Luigi Pirandello, *Six Characters in Search of an Author.* Bela Bartok, *Bluebeard's Castle.* Giacomo Puccini, *Il Trittico.* Gustav Cassel, *Theory of Social Economy.*

YEAR	AGE	THE LIFE AND THE LAND
1919	54	13 Jan: Marie Adelaide of Luxembourg abdicates.
		15 Jan: Accession of Marie Adelaide's sister Charlotte as Grand Duchess.
		11 Feb: Belgium's day before the Council of Ten.
		8 Mar: The Council of Ten agrees to revise 1839 Treaties.
		19 Mar: Belgian Commission report.
		4 Apr: King Albert's meeting with the Council of Four.
		16 Apr: The Council of Four approve Belgian Commission report, as amended.
		24 Apr: First Belgian-Luxembourgeois talks on economic union.
		29 Apr: The Council of Four concede Belgian reparations priority.
		1 May: The Council of Four accept Belgian reparations privilege in principle.
		4 May: Belgium accepts Versailles Treaty.
		19 May: Conference of Seven meets.
		30 May: Ruanda-Urundi transferred to Belgium.
		4 Jun: Great Powers exclude Dutch territorial transfer or international servitudes.
		18–19 Jun: Wilson visits Belgium.
		24 Jun: Formal agreement on Belgian priority.
		29 Jul: Commission of Fourteen meets.
		28 Sep: Luxembourg plebiscites.

YEAR	HISTORY	CULTURE
1919	Communist Revolt in Berlin.	Bauhaus movement founded by Walter Gropius.
	Benito Mussolini founds Fascist movement in Italy.	Wassily Kandinsky, *Dreamy Improvisation*.
	Britain and France authorise resumption of commercial relations with Germany.	Paul Klee, *Dream Birds*.
	British-Persian agreement at Tehran to preserve integrity of Persia.	Thomas Hardy, *Collected Poems*.
		Herman Hesse, *Demian*.
	Irish War of Independence begins.	George Bernard Shaw, *Heartbreak House*.
	US Senate vetoes ratification of Versailles Treaty leaving US outside League of Nations.	Eugene D'Albert, *Revolutionshochzeit*.
		Edward Elgar, *Concerto in E Minor for Cello*.
		Manuel de Falla, *The Three-Cornered Hat*.
		Film: *The Cabinet of Dr Caligari*.

YEAR	AGE	THE LIFE AND THE LAND
1920	55	16 Jan: League of Nations Council meets.
		23 Mar: Dutch claim Wielingen Channel; last meeting of Commission of Fourteen.
		14 Apr: Belgium joins French occupation of Frankfurt after Germany sends troops into Rhenish demilitarised zone.
		18–26 Apr: San Remo Conference.
		26 May: Franco-Belgian agreement on administration of Luxembourg railways.
		21–22 Jun: Boulogne Conference.
		1–3 Jul: Brussels Conference.
		5–16 Jul: Spa Conference.
		12 Jul: Lloyd George refuses to join Franco-Belgian military accord.
		29 Jul: Franco-Belgian military accord signed.
		28 Aug: Hymans resigns as Foreign Minister.
		7 Sep: Definitive version of Franco-Belgian military accord.
		15 Nov: League of Nations Assembly meets, Hymans presiding.
1921	56	20 Mar: Upper Silesia plebiscite.
		17 May: Belgian-Luxembourgeois customs union.
1922	57	Hymans President of League of Nations Council.
		6 Nov: Belgian-German protocol on Eupen-Malmédy railway.
1923	58	11 Jan: Ruhr encirclement.

YEAR	HISTORY	CULTURE
1920	Warren G Harding wins US Presidential election. Bolsheviks win Russian Civil War. Government of Ireland Act passed. Adolf Hitler announces his 25-point programme in Munich.	F Scott Fitzgerald, *This Side of Paradise.* Franz Kafka, *The Country Doctor.* Katherine Mansfield, *Bliss.* Rambert School of Ballet formed in London.
1921	Paris Conference of wartime Allies fixes Germany's reparation payments. Washington Naval Treaty signed.	D H Lawrence, *Women in Love.*
1922	Chanak crisis. League of Nations Council approves British Mandate in Palestine.	T S Eliot, *The Waste Land.* James Joyce, *Ulysses.* F Scott Fitzgerald, *The Beautiful and Damned.* Hermann Hesse, *Siddartha.*
1923	Adolf Hitler's *coup d'état* (Beer Hall Putsch) fails.	P G Wodehouse, *The Inimitable Jeeves.*

YEAR	AGE	THE LIFE AND THE LAND
1924	59	11 Mar: Hymans becomes Foreign Minister. 16 Jul–16 Aug: London Reparations Conference.
1925	60	3 Apr: Dutch-Belgian Treaty (not ratified). 13 May: Hymans leaves Foreign Ministry. 11 Aug: US-Belgian debt agreement. 16 Oct: Locarno Treaties.
1926	61	20 May: Hymans becomes Minister of Justice. 27 May: Collective Great Power Treaty (unratified) re Belgian-Dutch Treaty. 17 Sep: Briand-Stresemann meeting at Thoiry re possible Versailles Treaty revision.
1927	62	22 Nov: Hymans becomes Foreign Minister again.
1928	63	23 Feb: Franco-Belgian Economic Treaty. 27 Aug: Kellogg-Briand Pact signed. 16 Sep: Geneva communiqué on reparations and Rhineland.

YEAR	HISTORY	CULTURE
1924	Lenin dies. Dawes Plan published. Turkish National Assembly expels Ottoman dynasty.	Noel Coward, *The Vortex.* E M Forster, *A Passage to India.*
1925	Mussolini announces he will take dictatorial powers in Italy. Paul von Hindenburg elected President of Germany.	Noel Coward, *Hay Fever.* Franz Kafka, *The Trial.* Film: *Battleship Potemkin.*
1926	General Strike in Britain. Germany applies for admission to League of Nations; blocked by Spain and Brazil. Germany admitted to League of Nations; Spain leaves as result. Leon Trotsky and Grigory Zinoviev expelled from Politburo of Communist Party following Stalin's victory in USSR.	Franz Kafka, *The Castle.* A A Milne, *Winnie the Pooh.* Ernest Hemingway, *The Sun Also Rises.* Sean O'Casey, *The Plough and The Stars.* Film: *The General.*
1927	Inter-Allied military control of Germany ends.	Virginia Woolf, *To the Lighthouse.* Film: *The Jazz Singer.*
1928	Plebiscite in Germany against building new battleships fails.	D H Lawrence, *Lady Chatterley's Lover.* George Gershwin, *An American in Paris.* Kurt Weill, *The Threepenny Opera.*

YEAR	AGE	THE LIFE AND THE LAND
1929	64	7 Jun: Young Plan.
		13 Jul: Belgian-German marks accord.
		6–31 Aug: First Hague Conference.
		5 Sep: Hymans' speech on economic disarmament, Geneva.
		6 Sep: Briand speech on economic union, Geneva.
1930	65	3–20 Jan: Second Hague Conference
		30 Jun: Rhineland evacuation.
		14 Sep: Reichstag election.
		22 Dec: Oslo Convention.
1931	66	4 Mar: Hymans statement to Chamber on Belgian policy.
1932	67	2 Feb: Geneva Disarmament Conference opens.
		3 Mar: Special League Assembly on Manchuria, Hymans presiding.
		16 Jun–9 Jul: Lausanne Reparations Conference.
		20 Jun: Ouchy Convention.
1933	68	24 Feb: Special League Assembly endorses Lytton Report on Manchuria.
		12 Jun–27 Jul: London World Economic Conference.

YEAR	HISTORY	CULTURE
1929	Dictatorship established in Yugoslavia under King Alexander I; constitution suppressed. Fascists win single-party elections in Italy. Arabs attack Jews in Palestine following dispute over Jewish use of Wailing Wall. Wall Street Crash.	Ernest Hemingway, *A Farewell to Arms*. Erich Maria Remarque, *All Quiet on the Western Front*.
1930	Britain, France, Italy, Japan and US sign London Naval Treaty regulating naval expansion.	W H Auden, *Poems*. Noel Coward, *Private Lives*.
1931	Austrian Credit-Anstalt bankruptcy begins Central Europe's financial collapse.	William Faulkner, *Sanctuary*. Films: *Dracula. Little Caesar*.
1932	Chancellor Heinrich Brüning declares Germany cannot and will not resume reparation payments. Franklin D Roosevelt wins US Presidential election.	Aldous Huxley, *Brave New World*. Pablo Picasso, *Head of a Woman*. Films: *Grand Hotel. Tarzan the Ape Man*.
1933	Hitler becomes German Chancellor. Anglo-German Trade Agreement. Japan leaves League of Nations. Britain, France, Germany and Italy sign diluted version of Mussolini's proposed Four-Power Pact. Germany leaves League and Disarmament Conference.	George Orwell, *Down and Out in Paris and London*. Films: *Duck Soup. King Kong. Queen Christina*.

YEAR	AGE	THE LIFE AND THE LAND
1934	69	23 Feb: Accession of Leopold III.
		29 May: Disarmament Conference ends (except bureau).
		12 Jun: Hymans leaves Foreign Ministry.
		20 Nov: Hymans again Foreign Minister.
1935	70	25 Mar: Hymans leaves Foreign Ministry (last time); Hymans member of van Zeeland Cabinet without portfolio.
1936	71	6 Mar: Franco-Belgian military accord abrograted.
		7 Mar: Germany remilitarises Rhineland.
		19 Mar : Franco-Belgian-British London accord pending a new Locarno.
		24 May: Belgian election; Hymans re-elected; three-party coalition under van Zeeland formed.
		13 Jun: Hymans retires from Cabinet.
		14 Oct: King Leopold's statement to Cabinet on avoiding war.
1937	72	24 Apr: Anglo-French guarantee of Belgium (without obligation).

YEAR	HISTORY	CULTURE
1934	Germany: 'Night of the Long Knives'; role of German President and Chancellor merged, Hitler becomes *Führer* after German President Paul von Hindenburg dies.	F Scott Fitzgerald, *Tender Is the Night*. Robert Graves, *I, Claudius*. Film: *David Copperfield*.
1935	Saarland incorporated into Germany following plebiscite. British King George V's Silver Jubilee. Hoare-Laval Pact. Italy invades Abyssinia.	George Gershwin, *Porgy and Bess*. Films: *The 39 Steps. Top Hat.*
1936	British King George V dies: succeeded by Edward VIII, who abdicates at end of year to marry Wallis Simpson; succeeded by George VI. Franco mutiny in Morocco and throughout Spain starting Spanish Civil War. Mussolini proclaims Rome-Berlin Axis. Germany and Japan sign Anti-Comintern Pact against international communism.	J M Keynes, *General Theory of Employment, Interest and Money*. Berlin Olympics. Films: *Modern Times. Camille. The Petrified Forest. Things to Come* BBC begins world's first television transmission service.
1937	Italy joins German-Japanese Anti-Comintern Pact.	George Orwell, *The Road to Wigan Pier*.

YEAR	AGE	THE LIFE AND THE LAND
1940	75	10 May: Germany invades Belgium.
		18 May: Germany annexes Eupen-Malmédy.
		20 May: Belgian governments arrives in Le Havre.
1941	75	6 Mar: Hymans dies in Nice.

YEAR	HISTORY	CULTURE
1940	Second World War: Norwegian campaign failure causes Neville Chamberlain to resign: Winston Churchill becomes Britain's Prime Minister. Italy declares war on France and Britain. Battle of Britain.	Graham Greene, *The Power and the Glory.* Films: *The Great Dictator. Pinocchio. Rebecca.*
1941	Second World War: Germany invades USSR.	Noel Coward, *Blithe Spirit.*

Further Reading

Note: Multi-volume document collections, unpublished materials, articles in scholarly journals and works in languages other than English and French are excluded.

Primary Sources

Stephen B Wickham, *Belgium: a country study*, 2nd ed (US Department of the Army, Washington: 1985) is useful for general background. *Luxembourg* (Great Britain, Admiralty, Naval Intelligence Division, His Majesty's Stationery Office: 1944) is a helpful compendium, as is the companion volume *The Netherlands* (HMSO: 1944). Albert Nothumb (ed), *Le Luxembourg-Livre de Centenaire* (Imprimerie Saint Paul, Luxembourg: 1948), issued by the Grand Ducal government, is nicely done.

The Peace Conference debates of the Council of Four are eminently readable and give a good feel for the decision-making process. They are available in three editions: Paul Mantoux, *Les Déliberations du conseil des quatre (24 mars-28 juin 1919)*, 2 Volumes (Editions du centre national de la recherche scientifique: 1955); Paul Mantoux, *Paris Peace Conference, 1919: Proceedings of the Council of Four*, tr John

Boardman Whitton (Librarie Droz, Geneva: 1964), abridged; and Arthur S Link (ed), *The Deliberations of the Council of Four (March 24 – June 28 1919), Notes of the Official Interpreter, Paul Mantoux,* 2 Volumes (Princeton UP, Princeton: 1992).

Memoirs of the Peace Conference and the post-war years abound. Only a few can be mentioned. Most important are Paul Hymans' *Mémoires*, 2 Volumes, posthumously edited by Frans van Kalken and John Bartier (Éditions de l'Institut de Sociologie Solvay, Brussels: 1958) which focus exclusively on diplomatic and royal matters. Charles d'Ydewalle, *D'Albert I à Léopold III: Les Belges de mon Temps* (Editions Erel, Ostend: 1966) gives a better brief picture of the man and of other key Belgians. See also Emile Vandervelde, *Souvenirs d'un militant socialiste* (Les Éditions Denoël, Paris: 1939). Hugh Gibson, *A Journal from our Legation in Belgium* (Doubleday Page, Garden City NY: 1917), by the First Secretary, is important for wartime events, as is General Raoul van Overstraeten, *The War Diaries of Albert I, King of the Belgians* (William Kimber, London: 1954). Joseph Brand Whitlock, *The Letters and Journal of Brand Whitlock,* Allan Nevins (ed), 2 Volumes (Appleton-Century Co, New York: 1936) is extremely helpful for 1914–21, when Whitlock was the US envoy to Belgium. Stephen Bonsal, aide to Colonel House at the Peace Conference, published two useful volumes: *Unfinished Business* (Doubleday Doran, Garden City, New York: 1944) and *Suitors and Supplicants: The Little Nations at Versailles* (Prentice-Hall, New York: 1946). Anthony Eden (Earl of Avon), *The Memoirs of Anthony Eden: Facing the Dictators* (Houghton Mifflin, Boston: 1962) contributes on League of Nations matters.

Secondary Works

Sweeping general surveys, some from prehistory, of the Benelux countries, individually and collectively, include Paul Arblaster, *A History of the Low Countries* (Palgrave, Basingstoke: 2006), which covers all three states well. Henri Bernard, *Terre commune* (Brepols, Brussels: 1961) does the same. Equally sweeping but with obvious limitations is James Newcomer, *The Grand Duchy of Luxembourg* (University Press of America, Lanham, Maryland: 1984), E H Kossman, *The Low Countries, 1780–1940* (Clarendon Press, Oxford: 1978) is better on Holland than on Belgium, whereas J C H Blom and E Lamberts (eds), *History of the Low Countries*, tr James C Kennedy (Berghahn, New York: 2006 ed) is the reverse. Bernard A Cook, *Belgium: A History* (Peter Lang, New York: 2004) and Georges-Henri Dumont, *Histoire de la Belgique* (Le Cri, Brussels: 2000) are both clear and start from prehistory.

Among surveys focused on the 19th and 20th centuries, George Thomas Kurian, *The Benelux Countries* (Facts on File, New York: 1989) is clear and easy to use but scants history. Stephen Holt, *Six European States* (Hamish Hamilton, London: 1970) explains government structures of the Benelux countries and others. Martin Conway and Peter Romijn, 'Belgium and the Netherlands' in Robert Gerwarth (ed), *Twisted Paths: Europe 1914–1945* (Oxford UP, Oxford: 2007) deals with inter-war politics. Jan-Albert Goris, *Belgium* (University of California Press, Berkeley: 1946) addresses various aspects of the country, as does the companion volume, Bartholomew Landheer, *The Netherlands* (University of California Press, Berkeley: 1943). Amry Vanderbosch, *Dutch Foreign Policy since 1815* (Nijhoff, The Hague: 1959) is valuable. Frank E Huggett, *Modern Belgium* (Praeger, New York: 1969) is balanced and deals with diplomacy. Els Witte,

Jan Craeybeckx and Alain Meynen, *Political History of Belgium from 1830 onwards*, tr Raf Casert (Standaard Uitgeverij, Antwerp: 2000) is weak on foreign policy and awkward in its prose. Jonathan E Helmreich, *Belgium and Europe: A Study in Small Power Diplomacy* (Mouton, The Hague: 1976) is important and archivally based, as is Daniel H Thomas's very scarce *The Guarantee of Belgian Independence and Neutrality in European Diplomacy, 1830s–1930s* (D H Thomas Publishing, Kingston RI: 1983). Theo Aronson, *The Coburgs of Belgium* (Cassell, London: 1968) is entertaining and generally sound.

A serviceable summary of the First World War may be found in Spencer C Tucker, *The Great War, 1914–1918* (Indiana UP, Bloomington: 1998). Amry Vanderbosch, *The Neutrality of the Netherlands during the World War* (W B Eerdmans, Grand Rapids, Michigan: 1927) is solid. Maartje M Abbenhuis, *The Art of Staying Neutral: The Netherlands in the First World War* (Amsterdam UP, Amsterdam: 2006) concentrates on the domestic scene, as does Sophie de Schaepdrijver, *La Belgique et la première guerre mondiale* (Peter Lang, Brussels: 2004), which offers fine excellent depictions of wartime Belgium. John N Horne and Alan Kramer, *German Atrocities, 1914: a History of Denial* (Yale UP, New Haven: 2001) is definitive. Larry Zuckerman, *The Rape of Belgium* (New York UP, New York: 2004) has a somewhat broader focus. Commandant Adrien Gerlache de Gomery, *Belgium in Wartime*, tr Bernard Miall (George H Doran, New York: 1916) has useful details, especially on Sainte-Adresse, whereas Jean Massart, *The Secret Press in Belgium* (E P Dutton, New York: 1918) contains excerpts in English.

The literature of the Paris Peace Conference is enormous. Key works include Manfred F Boemeke, Gerald D Feldman and Elisabeth Glaser (eds), *The Treaty of Versailles: A Reassessment After 75 Years* (German Historical Institute, Washington DC and Cambridge UP, Cambridge: 1998) for recent scholarship; Inga Floto, *Colonel House in Paris* (Princeton UP, Princeton, New Jersey: 1980); and Harold I Nelson, *Land and Power* (David & Charles, Newton Abbott: 1971). Margaret Macmillan, *Paris, 1919* (Random House, New York: 2002) is entertaining. The best short treatment is Alan Sharp, *The Versailles Settlement: Peacemaking in Paris, 1919* (Macmillan, Basingstoke: 1991); see also his work in this series. William R Keylor (ed), *The Legacy of the Great War* (Houghton Mifflin, Boston: 1998) is a useful collection. The only study of Belgium at the Peace Conference is Sally Marks, *Innocent Abroad: Belgium at the Paris Peace Conference of 1919* (University of North Carolina Press, Chapel Hill: 1981).

For summaries of European international politics, 1918–33, the short version is Sally Marks, *The Illusion of Peace: International Relations in Europe, 1918–1933*, 2nd ed (Palgrave, Basingstoke: 2003); the brilliant detailed study is Zara Steiner, *The Lights that Failed: European International History, 1919–1933* (Oxford UP, Oxford: 2005). For the pre-war era, see P M H Bell, *The Origins of the Second World War in Europe* (Longmans, London: 1986). Of three surveys of interwar Belgian diplomacy, Jane Kathryn Miller, *Belgian Foreign Policy between Two Wars, 1919–1940* (Bookman Associates, New York: 1951) is still worth reading. Fernand van Langenhove, *La Belgique en quête de sécurité* (La Renaissance du livre, Brussels: 1969) is based entirely on the official five-volume *Documents diplomatiques belges, 1920–1940*. Baron Pierre van Zuylen, *Les Mains libres: politique extérieure de la Belgique, 1914–1940* (l'Édition universelle, Brussels: 1950) is an account by a Foreign Ministry participant in events.

Most important among biographies of Belgians is Robert Fenaux, *Paul Hymans, un homme, un temps* (Office de publicité, Brussels: 1946). Auguste Vierset and Oscar E Millard, *Burgomaster Max* (Hutchinson, London: 1936), by Max's chief of staff, is of limited use. Henri Haag, *Le Comte Charles de Broqueville*, 2 Volumes (Éditions Nauwelaerts, Brussels: 1990) is very detailed on the First World War. Janet Polasky, *The Democratic Socialism of Emile Vandervelde* (Berg, Oxford: 1995) focuses on socialism, not diplomacy. Liane Ranieri, *Emile Francqui* (Éditions Duculot, Paris: 1985) is a good portrait of a many-faceted man. Georges Sion, *Henri Jaspar, portrait d'un homme d'état* (Brepols, Brussels: 1964) is a brief sketch of a leader deserving a larger study. No biography of Georges Theunis has yet been published. Edith O'Shaughnessy, *Marie Adelaide: Grand Duchess of Luxembourg* (Harrison Smith, New York: 1932) is hagiographic.

Most helpful on the role of Hymans at the League of Nations are Margaret E Burton, *The Assembly of the League of Nations* (University of Chicago Press, Chicago: 1941); F P Walters (a former League official), *A History of the League of Nations*, 1 volume ed (Oxford UP, Oxford: 1960); and Elmer Bendiner, *A Time for Angels: The Tragicomic History of the League of Nations* (Knopf, New York: 1975). See also F S Northedge, *The League of Nations, its Life and Times, 1920–1946* (Holmes & Meier, New York: 1986) and Ruth B Henig (ed), *The League of Nations* (Barnes & Noble, New York: 1973) as well as her volume in this series.

There are a number of specialised studies of aspects of Belgium's problems. R Ahmann, A M Birke and M Howard (eds), *The Quest for Stability: Problems of West European Security, 1918–1957* (German Historical Institute, London, and Oxford UP, Oxford: 1993) contains Ger van Roon,

'Neutrality and Security: The Experience of the Oslo States' and Zara Steiner, 'The League of Nations and the Quest for Security'. Martin S Alexander, *The Republic in Danger* (Cambridge UP, New York: 1992) is excellent on Franco-Belgian military relations. Astrid von Busekist, *La Belgique: Politique des langues et construction de l'état de 1780 à nos jours* (Duculot, Paris: 1998) is a scholarly approach to the language question. Éric Bussière, *La France, la Belgique et l'organisation économique de l'Europe, 1918–1935* (Comité pour l'histoire économique et financière de la France, Paris: 1992) is by a Frenchman with a Belgian viewpoint. Christian Calmes, *Le Luxembourg au centre de l'annexionnisme belge, 1914–1919* (Imprimerie Saint-Paul, Luxembourg: 1976) is detailed but unreliable. Rolande Depoortere, *La question des reparations allemandes dans la politique étrangère de la Belgique après la première guerre mondiale, 1919–1925* (Académie royale de Belgique, Brussels: 1997) does a fine job with a difficult subject. Kas Depres and Louis Vos (eds), *Nationalism in Belgium* (Macmillan, New York: 1998) is helpful on the German minority. Manfred J Enssle, *Stresemann's Territorial Revisionism* (Franz Steiner Verlag, Wiesbaden: 1980) analyses the questions of Eupen-Malmédy and the paper marks. David Owen Kieft, *Belgium's Return to Neutrality* (Clarendon Press, Oxford: 1972) is the able standard work on the decisions of 1936. Wm Roger Louis, *Ruanda-Urundi, 1884–1919* (Clarendon Press, Oxford: 1963) is another able standard work. Sally Marks, 'The Belgo-German Border, 1914–1956' may be found in Christian Baechler and Carole Fink (eds), *The Establishment of European Frontiers after Two World Wars* (Peter Lang, Bern: 1996). Richard H Meyer, *Bankers' Diplomacy* (Columbia UP, New York: 1970) addresses Belgian financial problems whereas

Robert L Rothstein, *Alliances and Small Powers* (Columbia UP, New York: 1968) deals with the Franco-Belgian military accord. Stephen A Schuker, *The End of French Predominance in Europe* (University of North Carolina Press, Chapel Hill: 1976) is essential on the Dawes Plan and the 1924 London Conference. Gilbert Trausch, 'Les relations franco-belges à propos de la question luxembourgeois (1914–1922)' in Actes du Colloque de Metz, *Les relations franco-belges de 1830 à 1934* (Metz UP, Metz: 1975) is very fine. H van der Wee and K Tavernier, *La Banque Nationale de Belgique et l'histoire monétaire entre deux guerres mondiales* (Banque Nationale de Belgique, Brussels: 1975) is narrowly focused but useful on the crises of 1926 and 1935.

Picture Sources

The author and publishers wish to express their thanks to the following sources of illustrative material and/or permission to reproduce it. They will make proper acknowledgements in future editions in the event that any omissions have occurred.

Photographic illustration courtesy of Corbis and Topham Picturepoint.

Endpapers
The Signing of Peace in the Hall of Mirrors, Versailles, 28th June 1919 by Sir William Orpen (Imperial War Museum: Bridgeman Art Library)
Front row: Dr Johannes Bell (Germany) signing with Herr Hermann Müller leaning over him
Middle row (seated, left to right): General Tasker H Bliss, Col E M House, Mr Henry White, Mr Robert Lansing, President Woodrow Wilson (United States); M Georges Clemenceau (France); Mr David Lloyd George, Mr Andrew Bonar Law, Mr Arthur J Balfour, Viscount Milner, Mr G N Barnes (Great Britain); Prince Saionji (Japan)

Back row (left to right): M Eleftherios Venizelos (Greece);
Dr Afonso Costa (Portugal); Lord Riddell (British Press);
Sir George E Foster (Canada); M Nikola Pašić (Serbia);
M Stephen Pichon (France); Col Sir Maurice Hankey,
Mr Edwin S Montagu (Great Britain); the Maharajah of
Bikaner (India); Signor Vittorio Emanuele Orlando (Italy);
M Paul Hymans (Belgium); General Louis Botha (South
Africa); Mr W M Hughes (Australia)

Jacket images

(Front): Imperial War Museum: akg Images.
(Back): *Peace Conference at the Quai d'Orsay* by Sir William
Orpen (Imperial War Museum: akg Images).
Left to right (seated): Signor Orlando (Italy); Mr Robert
Lansing, President Woodrow Wilson (United States); M
Georges Clemenceau (France); Mr David Lloyd George, Mr
Andrew Bonar Law, Mr Arthur J Balfour (Great Britain);
Left to right (standing): M Paul Hymans (Belgium); Mr
Eleftherios Venizelos (Greece); The Emir Feisal (The
Hashemite Kingdom); Mr W F Massey (New Zealand);
General Jan Smuts (South Africa); Col E M House (United
States); General Louis Botha (South Africa); Prince Saionji
(Japan); Mr W M Hughes (Australia); Sir Robert Borden
(Canada); Mr G N Barnes (Great Britain); M Ignacy
Paderewski (Poland)

Index

Makers of the Modern World

UK PUBLICATION: November 2008 to December 2010
CLASSIFICATION: Biography/History/
   International Relations
FORMAT: 198 × 128mm
EXTENT: 208pp
ILLUSTRATIONS: 6 photographs plus 4 maps
TERRITORY: world

Chronology of life in context, full index, bibliography innovative layout with sidebars